Other Regal Venture Books by Ethel Barrett
The Strangest Thing Happened...
Which Way to Nineveh?
The People Who Couldn't Be Stopped
The Secret Sign
I'm No Hero
Rules, Who Needs Them?
If I Had a Wish
God and a Boy Named Joe
God, Have You Got It All Together?

These Regal Venture books make Bible stories come alive for readers of every age. They also provide exciting resources for G/L pre-teens Bible studies.

ETHEL BARRETT
tells Bible Stories to children
Volume 1

A Division of G/L Publications
Glendale, California, U.S.A.

© Copyright 1977 by G/L Publications
All rights reserved

Published by
Regal Books Division, G/L Publications
Glendale, California 91209

Printed in U.S.A.
Library of Congress Catalog Card No. 76-45256
ISBN 0-8307-0474-6

Contents

Ways to Use This Book 7

PART I STORIES OF THE BEGINNINGS
Story 1   The World That Was "Just Right" 12
Story 2   The First Man 17
Story 3   The First Lie 22
Story 4   The Strangest Boat in the World 27
Story 5   The Strangest Boat Ride in the World 32
Story 6   Noah Says "Thank You" 37
Story 7   The Strange Journey 42
Story 8   A Selfish Choice 46
Story 9   The Visitors Who Made a Promise 50
Story 10 The Man Who Obeyed God No Matter WHAT 54
Story 11 The Hardest Test in the World 58
Story 12 How a Prayer Was Answered 62
Story 13 The Man Who Ran Away 67
Story 14 Two Brothers in Trouble 71
SONG "For Us All" 75

PART II STORIES OF JOSEPH

Story 15   The Gift That Caused Trouble   **78**
Story 16   The Dreams That Caused Trouble   **82**
Story 17   The Errand That Ended in Trouble   **86**
Story 18   The Journey That Changed a Life   **90**
Story 19   A Terrible Lie   **94**
Story 20   The Dream That Was Almost Forgotten   **98**
Story 21   The Dream That Set a Prisoner Free   **102**
Story 22   An Old Dream That Came True   **106**
Story 23   The Journey with Nine Surprises   **111**
Story 24   The Biggest Surprise of ALL   **115**
Story 25   The Best News of All   **120**
Story 26   A Wish That Came True   **124**
SONG   "God's Word"   **128**

When you see one of these (*) look at the bottom of the page.

WAYS TO USE THIS BOOK

"Read some more!" is one of the most rewarding compliments a listener can give, for it reflects his feelings of wanting to repeat a pleasant experience.

WHY READ TO A CHILD?

Listening to a good story, well read, has many values for a child. It helps him learn to listen and thus increases his attention span. Listening to a good story also helps him develop his ability to retain a sequence of ideas. As he talks with you about a story he has heard, he gains experience in speaking and thus increases his vocabulary. And when your child snuggles down beside you to hear a story, an emotional closeness develops from this warm and personal interaction.

WHY READ BIBLE STORIES?

Our purpose in reading Bible stories to a child is to share with him the gospel of God's love and the meaning of that love for everyone. It's also a way of telling a child that WE highly value what God says to us in the Bible.

Reading and talking about Bible stories provide natural value-teaching situations. For example, in Story 19, Joseph's brothers lie to their father, Jacob. This story offers a natural opportunity to talk about the way others feel when we are dishonest.

STORY READING TIPS

1. Read daily. It's vital to establish and maintain a regular story time. The length of time isn't as important as its regularity. Some parents make story reading a bedtime ritual. Others include story time as a part of family times.

2. Read expressively. Let your voice reflect your enthusiasm for what you're reading so that your genuine interest in the story comes through. You can add variety and maintain the child's attention if you add "sound effects" to the words you read. For example, ". . . the great ark cre-e-eaked and s-c-r-a-p-e-d—and—settled down and—came to a stop. It had landed—on a high mountaintop!"

Create excitement by speaking slightly faster. Whisper or pause briefly to add suspense. For example, ". . . While they traveled, Jacob thought, 'Esau—Esau—Esau—.' And the clop-clop of the camels' feet seemed to say, 'Eee—sau, Eee—sau, Eee—sau'—until, suddenly there off in the distance—Esau was coming! Esau came closer and closer and CLOSER—"

Change the tone of your voice to identify and reflect the feelings of the Bible story characters. For instance, " 'Joseph!' cried Jacob, hardly daring to believe his eyes . . . 'Father,

Father,' said Joseph, 'I could not wait. I had to come to meet you.' "

3. Read creatively. Young children, particularly, thrive on repetition. After your child has become quite familiar with a story, omit a word and let him "fill in the blank." Of course, the word should be an important one, such as an action word or a person's name.

4. Follow the story with fun-to-do activities. Include the "Let's Talk About the Bible Story" section (following each story) to help clarify ideas presented in the story; to discuss how story characters may have felt; and to think of how we might have felt in a similar situation. Take turns answering the questions to avoid a "test" atmosphere. Or, you might let each listener ask another family member one question about the story.

Provide appropriate art materials for your child to use in drawing or painting a picture of his favorite part of the story.

Help your child learn to repeat with understanding the Bible verse given at the conclusion of the "Let's Talk About" section. Talk together about the meaning of the verse. Ask, "What is another way to say this verse? . . ." Show your child where the verse is printed in the Bible. Let him underline with a red pencil the verse in his Bible (to help him locate it easily).

A child who is learning to use his Bible will be interested in finding the story for himself. Guide him in locating the story in relation to the Old and New Testaments; also in relation to adjacent books in the Bible.

Sing together the songs included in this book (see "Contents") as a part of your fun-to-do activities.

PART ONE
STORIES OF THE BEGINNINGS

STORY 1

THE WORLD THAT WAS "JUST RIGHT"

Did you ever watch your mother bake a cake? She doesn't make it just any old way, does she? She puts in just the RIGHT things at the RIGHT time. If she put paint in her mixing bowl instead of chocolate, the cake might LOOK pretty but it wouldn't be good. A cake has to be made just right. It has to be made according to a recipe. It has to be made according to a plan.

Once there was a world. And it didn't just happen. It was made. It was made according to a PLAN.

In the very beginning of the Bible it tells us that God made the world. He did! And He didn't make it just any old way either. It had to be made just right. So first He planned it. And then He made it—oh, a long, LONG time ago. He put everything in its place and it was all JUST RIGHT. And this is what He did.

The first thing God did was make the light. He made it by just SAYING, "Let there be light." God tells us so in the Bible. Now of course it isn't very good for it to be light ALL the time, because nobody would get any SLEEP—so God made it light on PART of the time. He separated the light from the darkness, and He called the light "day." And He called the darkness "night." But the world wasn't finished yet. It needed more. And God DID more.

The second day He said, "Let there be a sky." And there was! He stretched it out overhead, blue and beautiful. The Bible says "He stretches out the sky like a curtain." So now the world had day and night—and a sky. But it wasn't finished yet. It needed more. Do you know why? It was all water! Everywhere, all over, every BIT of it was water. Now of course THAT wasn't the way God wanted it. It needed MUCH more than that. And God DID more.

The third day God gathered the water together and separated it from the land. Oh there was a LOT of water. Enough to make great big oceans. Enough to make rivers and lakes. And enough left over to make little creeks. God put the oceans and the rivers and the lakes and the creeks right where He wanted them. And He made them stay right there in their places. He even made the mighty ocean stay in its place, just as if it were a baby. "This far you may go," He said, "and this far—but no farther." And the ocean has been obeying God ever since, which is a very good thing, when you stop to think that if the ocean just BURPS, we have a tidal wave.

Then God spoke to the seeds that He had put into the dry land, and He said, "Grow." And they did! Some grew just to make things beautiful—like the lovely flowers and trees and grass and vines. And some grew things to eat—like vegetables and fruits and nuts and berries. Of course most things grew

UP—like corn and tomatoes and oranges and peas. But some things grew DOWN—like carrots and radishes. And some things grew SIDEWAYS—like vines creeping along the ground. But everything grew in SOME direction. And the earth began to look very beautiful.

On the fourth day, God hung out the sun and He hung out the moon and He hung out the stars. Oh that was a wonderful day! God tells us in the Bible that the "stars sang together for joy." God put each star in its own pathway, and He said, "Now, don't you get in the way of any other star." And the stars obeyed God, and each little star stayed in its own pathway. And God hung out the sun to shine in the daytime and the moon to shine at night. That was really a wonderful day.

At last God had finished nearly everything He wanted to make. The light and the darkness. The sky and the sun and the moon and the stars. The oceans and rivers and lakes and creeks. The dry land, the flowers and trees and vegetables and fruits.

After all these things were made, God looked at the beautiful world and He said, "It is GOOD."

That means it was JUST RIGHT.

Just the way a cake has to be made. According to a plan. Just right. That's the way God made the world.

Just right.

LET'S TALK ABOUT THE BIBLE STORY

How big is big? How big is bigger? Biggest? Do you know how big VAST* is?

Have you ever tried to think of the VASTNESS of the universe God created? Do you know that the sun is more than

---

* Vast is just about as big as you can imagine!

a million times bigger than earth? And that the nearest star seen at night is four light-years, or about twenty-four TRILLION miles, away? And that there are probably 200 BILLION stars in our galaxy, or group of stars? And that there are more than ten thousand galaxies, all hurtling through space at tremendous speed—and yet none of the stars bump into each other or get into each other's way?

How does it make you feel when you think of the greatness of our God, who created this vast universe and made everything in it just right?

A BIBLE VERSE TO LEARN

In the beginning God created the heaven and the earth. (Genesis 1:1, *KJV*)

Another verse you might like to learn: "O Lord God! You have made the heavens and earth by your great power; nothing is too hard for you!" (Jeremiah 32:17, *TLB*)

LET'S TALK TO GOD

Dear God, help us to understand how VAST the universe is, and how GREAT you are. And that you do EVERYTHING just right. It's wonderful to know that you are taking care of us. Thank you! In Jesus' name, Amen.

NOW FIND THIS STORY IN YOUR BIBLE
It's in Genesis 1:1–19.

STORY 2

THE FIRST MAN

God has made a wonderful world! Everything He had made was just right. The light and the darkness. The sky and the moon and the stars. The oceans and rivers and lakes. The dry land, and the flowers and the trees and vegetables and fruit. This was a wonderful world—

Except for one thing.

There were no living creatures in it!

There was all that water—and no fish to swim in it.

And all that beautiful sky—and no birds to fly in it.

And all those forests and fields and hills and valleys—and no animals to run and climb and play in them.

And this is what God did.

First He made the fishes. ALL the fishes. More fishes than you can even dream of!

>Tiny goldfishes and guppies
>and middle-sized fishes—
>and GREAT BIG fishes—
>like WHALE-SHARKS!

God said, "Let the oceans and lakes and rivers and creeks be FILLED with all kinds of fishes."

And they were!

The tiny fishes swam in the little brooks. The middle-sized fishes swam in the lakes and rivers. And EVERY kind of fish swam in the big oceans, from tiny ones to whale-sharks as long as some of our houses.

God made the fishes but that wasn't all. The next thing He made—was birds. So many birds! More birds than you can imagine!

>Tiny humming-birds
>and middle-sized birds—
>and GREAT BIG birds—
>like EAGLES and FLAMINGOS and
>PEACOCKS and even OSTRICHES!

And God said, "Let the birds fly across the sky—all over the earth!"

And they did!

Some birds flew around the trees and stayed in the little hills and valleys. Some birds—like the sea gulls—flew out over the water. And some BIG birds—like the eagle—flew to the highest mountaintops!

Now God had made the fishes and the birds, but STILL that wasn't all. The NEXT thing He made—was animals. More animals than you can even think of!

>Little mice and chipmunks—

and middle-sized dogs and pigs—
and GREAT BIG BEARS and LIONS and
TIGERS and even ELEPHANTS!

God said, "Let there be all kinds of animals—big ones and little ones and all sizes in between. And let them roam all over the earth."

And they did!

Some animals—like the alligator—stayed near the water. Some—like the monkeys—climbed the trees. And some just liked to get way off by themselves in the deep forest.

Now this was all very wonderful. Except for one thing.

There was nobody for God to talk to. Nobody to talk back to Him. Nobody in all this world for God to love with a SPECIAL love—and enjoy forever! So the next thing God did was the most wonderful of all. He said, "Let Us create MAN in our own image."

And that's exactly what He did!

God created man, and He called this man ADAM.

God let Adam live in this wonderful world. He let Adam take care of all the beautiful things. And He even let Adam give all the animals and birds their names! The Bible says that God brought all the beasts and the birds to Adam to see what he would call them. Adam named every bird, from the tiny hummingbirds to the great big peacocks. And every animal from the tiny chipmunks to the great big elephants. He gave every living creature its name!

Yes, Adam was created to care for all that God had made. But most important of all, God had somebody He could love with a SPECIAL love. And Adam loved God.

After all these things were done, God said, "It is good."

That means everything was JUST RIGHT.

Just the way the world was made. According to a plan.

Just right. That's the way God made the things IN the world. Just right.

LET'S TALK ABOUT THE BIBLE STORY

God had made a wonderful world—except for what? What did He do about it? What did He make first? What did He make second? And then what did He make? And what was STILL missing? Why did God want to make Adam? What did He let Adam do?

God loves YOU with a very special love—just as He loved Adam. And God wants you to talk to Him. How can you talk to God? What are some times you especially like to talk to God in prayer? What are some things you like to tell God?

A BIBLE VERSE TO LEARN

Know that the LORD Himself is God; it is He who has made us, and not we ourselves; we are His people and the sheep of His pasture. (Psalm 100:3, *NASB*)

LET'S TALK TO GOD

Dear God, we thank you that you made Adam because you wanted someone to love you. We thank you that you love US with a very SPECIAL love. And we love you, too. In Jesus' name, Amen.

NOW FIND THIS STORY IN YOUR BIBLE

It's in Genesis 1:20–31, Genesis 2: 1 to 3. Then 7 and 19.

STORY 3

THE FIRST LIE

God had been so good to Adam! He had made a wonderful world that was "just right." And He had given Adam a beautiful garden to live in. There were no signs that said "KEEP OFF THE GRASS" and no signs that said "DO NOT FEED THE ANIMALS." Adam could do anything he pleased—except ONE THING. He could not eat the fruit on ONE CERTAIN TREE. This tree was in the middle of the Garden. God knew it was best for Adam not to eat the fruit on this tree. He TOLD Adam. "Adam," He said, "this is the tree of the knowledge of good and evil, and if you eat that fruit, it will HURT you." Well THAT'S plain enough!

God had done MANY things for Adam, but He asked Adam to do just ONE thing for Him—to OBEY Him.

And God thought of everything to make Adam happy. He even made Adam a beautiful wife, and her name was Eve. So

now Adam had the Garden, the animals and the birds—and a wife!

Adam and Eve were so happy in the Garden—it didn't seem possible that anything could go wrong.

But something did. And it happened like this:

One day, Eve was walking in the Garden, when she came to the tree right in the middle—the tree that God had said not to eat from. Eve was looking at the fruit and thinking about it, when along came—a beautiful creature. This beautiful creature was a serpent.

And the serpent said to Eve, "Has God said that you must not eat the fruit from EVERY tree in the Garden?"

"Oh NO," said Eve, "God didn't say that at all. We can eat all the OTHER fruit. It's just the fruit on this ONE TREE that we should not eat. God said it would hurt us."

And that wicked serpent told the lie that started all the trouble. "It won't REALLY hurt you," he said slyly. "It will just make you WISE. You shall be as gods, knowing good and evil."

Well!

It SOUNDED so good that Eve believed it. First she picked some fruit. Then she ATE it. Then she gave Adam some. And HE ate it, too. And so they both disobeyed God.

Well, the MINUTE they disobeyed God, they began to be afraid. When God came to visit them, and they heard His voice in the Garden, they were so afraid that they HID.

"Adam," called God, "where are you?"

And Adam called back, "Lord, I was afraid when I heard your voice, and so I hid."

Now of course Adam and Eve couldn't REALLY hide from God. God knew right where they were. And He also knew that they had done the ONE THING He had told them NOT to do.

And because they had disobeyed Him, God told Adam and Eve to leave the Garden.

God still LOVED Adam and Eve. He loved them so much that He even went with them outside the Garden, to watch over them.

But nothing could be quite the same again. God had made a beautiful garden—but Adam and Eve had disobeyed—and spoiled it all!

LET'S TALK ABOUT THE BIBLE STORY

God asked Adam to do just ONE thing for him—what was it? What happened to Adam and Eve after they disobeyed God? What is one way God showed he still loved them? Can you think of some ways you have disobeyed and "spoiled it all"? The Bible calls it sin, and says that sin must be punished.

But the Bible has some wonderful news for you!

First, there's something you must do. It tells us what, in Psalm 38:18. ("I will be sorry for my sin.") And now comes the wonderful news. God has already sent his son Jesus to take your punishment! All you have to do is BELIEVE that. And then let him KNOW you believe it. Tell him you want to belong to him. For the Bible says that "God so loved the world (that means you) that he gave his son . . . that whosoever (that means you again) BELIEVES in him . . . shall have everlasting life." (John 3:16) After you've done this, do you know who you are? Why, you're a child of God! Isn't THAT wonderful news?

A BIBLE VERSE TO LEARN

But as many as received Him, to them He gave the right to become children of God, even to those who believe in His name. (John 1:12, *NASB*)

LET'S TALK TO GOD

Dear God, thank you for sending Jesus to be our Saviour. Show us the wrong things we do. Help us to "be sorry for our sin" and obey your commands. Thank you for loving us so much. In Jesus' name, Amen.

NOW FIND THIS STORY IN YOUR BIBLE

It's in Genesis 2:20-25 and 3:1-24.

STORY 4

THE STRANGEST BOAT IN THE WORLD

Did you ever have all your friends go off to play somewhere you weren't allowed to go? Perhaps there was deep water nearby, or railroad tracks, or SOMETHING dangerous or wrong. And your friends ran off laughing and left you alone, and there you were, the only one on the whole street who was OBEYING. Sometimes it's lonely business, being the only one obeying. It might be LONELY. But it's RIGHT. And that's what counts with God!

There is one thing God wants, more than anything else in the world. He wants His children to love and obey Him.

He does!

Remember, Adam and Eve didn't obey God and they had to leave the beautiful Garden. But that wasn't all—

Adam and Eve had children, and their children had children, until after awhile—oh, it took a long time—but after awhile, the world was just FILLED with people who didn't obey God. NO ONE obeyed God—

Except for one man. He still talked to God, and prayed to God, and thanked God for everything. And he taught his family to know God and obey Him too! His name was Noah, and he had quite a family. He had a wife—Mrs. Noah; and three sons, and their wives—and their names were

    Mr. and Mrs. Shem,

        And Mr. and Mrs. Ham,

            And Mr. and Mrs. Japheth.

Now one day, Noah called his family around him, and he said, "Something very important is going to happen. God has been talking to me, and He has given me some plans."

"Plans?" said Noah's family. "What plans? Are they for a house? Are they for a castle?"

"No," said Noah. "They're not for a house. And they're not for a castle. They're for a BOAT. God calls it an ARK."

"An Ark?" they cried. "An ARK?" They could hardly believe their ears. "Why there isn't even any WATER around here. Why would God want you to build an ark?"

"God is very sad," said Noah. "And He's told me something that's very sad. God has told me that all the people are so wicked, that His beautiful world is spoiled. And He's going to have to destroy it. He's going to send a big flood."

A flood? A FLOOD?

Why, that was hard to believe. It was even hard to IMAGINE. Noah and his family just had to take God's word for it, and obey.

And they did.

They began to build a boat.

Now this was no ordinary job. It was a BIG job. For this was no ordinary boat. It was a BIG boat. It was bigger than that, even.

It was TREMENDOUS!

This ark had to be big enough for Noah and his whole family—and that wasn't all!

It had to be big enough to hold hundreds of animals and birds, and enough food to last for a long, long time.

Noah and his helpers got to work. The cut down big trees. They measured. The sawed—zzzz-schhhhhh-zzzz-schhhh. They fit pieces together. They hammered. They lifted and hammered some more—until they had built that great ark exactly as God had told them to.

It was three stories high.

   And 'most as big as a battleship.

      And it had a window, way up high, big enough

         so that plenty of air could get in.

Yes, building the ark was a big job, and it took a long time. But, finally, the ark was done.

People came to look at it, and went on their way again. They didn't care about the old ark, and they didn't care about God. And they didn't care about Noah. If they thought about him at all, it was to laugh at him.

But Noah didn't care.

He didn't care because he was busy obeying God. He didn't care if PEOPLE laughed. He knew GOD was pleased.

Because there is one thing God wants more than anything else. He wants his children to love Him and obey Him.

And that's just what Noah and his family had done.

LET'S TALK ABOUT THE BIBLE STORY

What does God want more than anything else? What did he

ask Noah to do? Why? Did the people care? Did GOD care? Did you ever get left alone, the only one OBEYING? How did you feel? Did you think God cared? How do you know God cares?

A BIBLE VERSE TO LEARN
We must obey God rather than men. (Acts 5:29, *NASB*)

LET'S TALK TO GOD
Dear God, we know that you want us to love and obey you, and to love and obey our parents. But God, sometimes it's HARD to obey when nobody ELSE is obeying. Please help us to obey, even though we're all alone. In Jesus' name, Amen.

NOW FIND THIS STORY IN YOUR BIBLE
It's in Genesis 6:5–22.

STORY 5

THE STRANGEST BOAT RIDE IN THE WORLD

Did you ever have to obey when it didn't make any SENSE? Suppose you were walking through the woods with your father and suddenly your father said, "Stand still! Don't more. Stand—absolutely—still." And you obeyed. But then nothing happened. And nothing happened. And nothing happened. And THEN—

Your father took a big stick—and went—slowly—over—to—the—side—of—the—path—and—WHAM! killed a rattlesnake! THEN you'd know what it was all about. And THEN you'd be glad you had obeyed.

Sometimes we have to obey even when we don't understand and even when nothing happens!

Noah obeyed God.

The ark that God had told Noah to make was finished. And now Noah was ready to begin the NEXT step of his important job. And if building the huge ark was hard, this next step was even harder.

For God had told him to gather animals to put in the ark. Not just any old animals. And not just a FEW animals. But a father and a mother of EVERY KIND of animal in the land. And that wasn't all.

Noah had to gather FOURTEEN of certain special animals. And that wasn't all.

He had to have food and water enough for all the animals and for his family too.

Believe me, that meant a lot of animals and a lot of food. It was a BIG job.

Well, Noah did exactly as God had told him to do. He took two mice, two dogs, two lions, two elephants—

Two hummingbirds, two robins, two peacocks. Two—

From the littlest to the biggest, there wasn't one single kind of animal or bird or insect left out.

That wasn't easy!

But at last everything was ready. And then—

God told Noah and his family—

Mrs. Noah—

   Mr. and Mrs. Shem—

      Mr. and Mrs. Ham—

         —and Mr. and Mrs. Japheth—

—to go into the ark, and to bring with them all the animals and all the birds that they had gathered together.

Now it hadn't started to rain yet. But Noah didn't wait around to see if it would rain. He obeyed God. The Bible tells us that THE SAME DAY Noah entered the ark with his family. And all the animals! What a sight that must have been!

Two chipmunks, two pigs, two tigers, two sparrows, two eagles, two monkeys, two giraffes, two pigeons, two squirrels, two—

From the littlest to the BIGGEST, two of every kind. And fourteen of certain SPECIAL kinds. That line of animals just went on and on and on and on and ON.

It took a long time. But after a while Noah and his family and the animals were all safe in the ark. And then—

The Bible says, "God shut the door." And THEN—

Nothing happened. Absolutely nothing. Nothing happened and nothing happened and nothing happened. For seven whole days. And then—

RAIN!

Noah and his family heard the first sprinkles on the roof of the ark. Then they heard the rain coming down
>harder
>>and harder
>>>and HARDER.

The water began to slosh up along the bottom of the ark. It sloshed and sloshed and got deeper and DEEPER. And then that great big ark CREAKED—and SWAYED a bit—and then—

It—began—to—FLOAT.

It was going to be all right. Noah had followed every single direction in the plans God had given him, and the ark was watertight, and balanced right, and seaworthy.

The ark floated there in the clearing for several days. The rain came down day and night. On and on and on.

Inside the ark, Noah and his family had plenty to do. They took care of the animals and fed them, and they kept the ark clean. And every day they prayed, and thanked God for keeping them safe.

And that water got higher and HIGHER. After a while, only the treetops showed about the water. And after a long while, even the MOUNTAINTOPS were covered with water, and there was nothing left but water and sky. By this time, it had rained forty days and forty nights.

And then the rain stopped.

Now Noah didn't know what was going to happen next. Neither did Mrs. Noah. Nor Mr. and Mrs. Shem. Nor Mr. and Mrs. Ham. Nor Mr. and Mrs. Japeth. No one knew. But they weren't afraid.

The weren't afraid, because they DID know one thing. They had done exactly what God had told them to do. And God would keep them safe, for they had OBEYED.

LET'S TALK ABOUT THE BIBLE STORY

Is is hard for you to obey when you don't understand? Do you always know what your parents MEAN when they ask you to do something? Are there some things you can't do and you don't know WHY? How does this make you feel?

A BIBLE VERSE TO LEARN

When I am afraid, I will put my trust in (God). (Psalm 56:3, NASB)

LET'S TALK TO GOD

Dear God, sometimes it's hard to obey when we don't understand. Help us to trust you. And help us to know that you love us and care for us. And thank you for keeping us safe. In Jesus' name, Amen.

NOW FIND THIS STORY IN YOUR BIBLE

It's in Genesis 7:1–24.

STORY 6

NOAH SAYS "THANK YOU"

Next to loving him and obeying him, one thing God wants his children to do is THANK him.

And Noah and his family had plenty to thank God for. For even though there was absolutely nothing outside but water— they were all safe and snug inside the ark.

Days went by. Weeks went by. Months went by. One hundred and fifty days. Twenty weeks. Five months! And then, finally—

Wind!

Wind. Howling outside the ark. Racing across the water. Driving the water away. Making it go down faster. God hadn't forgotten them!

Indeed he hadn't. The Bible says, "And God REMEMBERED Noah and his family and all the animals that were

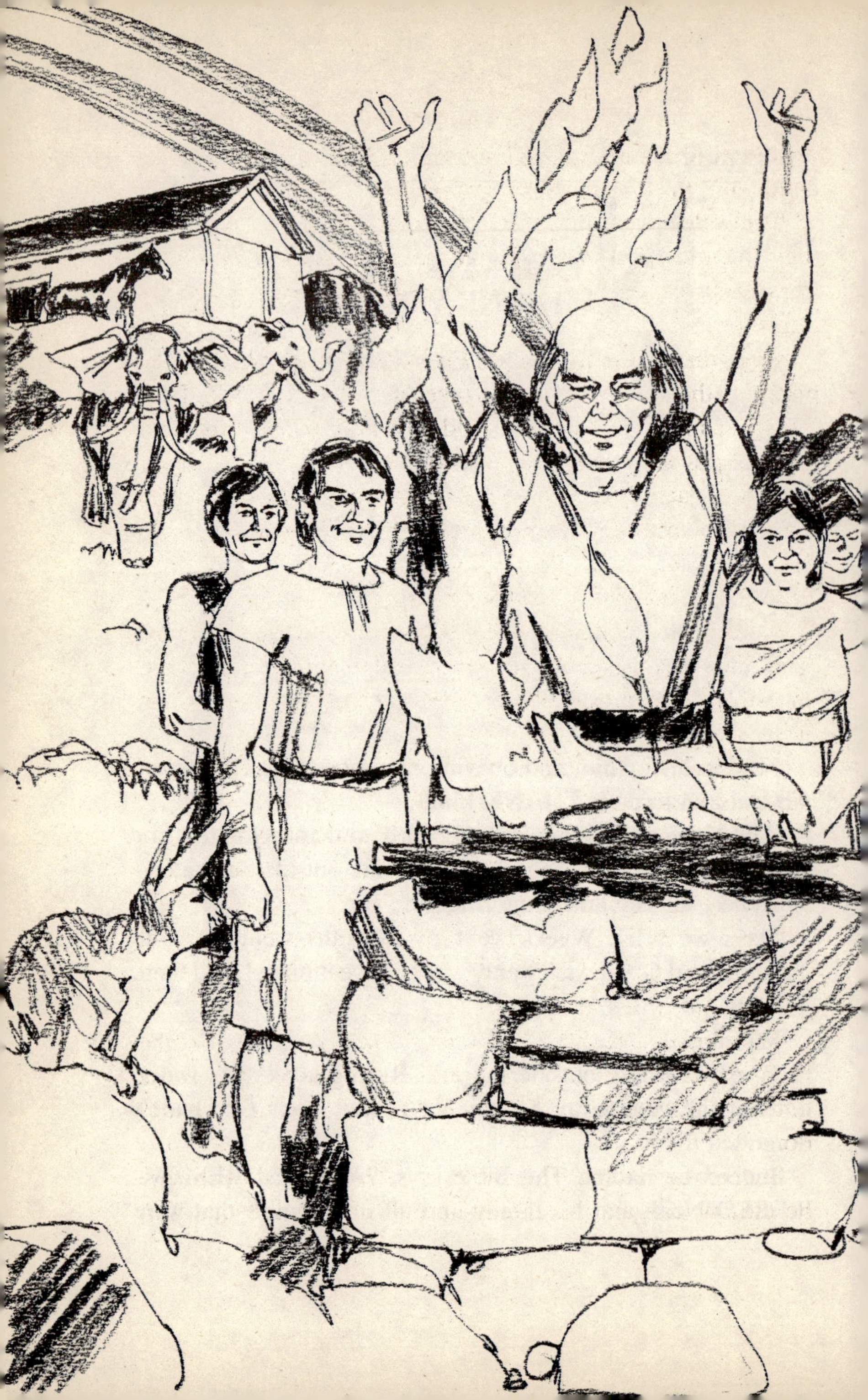

with him in the ark; and God made a wind to pass over the earth, and the waters began to go down."

The waters went down and down and DOWN—until, one day—the great ark cre-e-eaked and s-c-r-a-p-e-d—and—settled down and—came to a stop. It had landed—on a high mountaintop!

It was time to get busy at last. First Noah took a raven and let him out the window. But the raven never came back. Then Noah let a little dove out the window. The dove flew back and forth across the waters, and then came back!

A week later Noah let the little dove out the window again. She flew across the waters—and disappeared. But that evening she came back. And in her beak was a leaf from an olive tree! That meant the water had gone down below the treetops.

A week later, Noah let the little dove out the window again. This time she never came back. And they knew she had probably found a tree to build a nest in, and that most of the water had gone.

Noah and his sons got to work. They took the covering off the ark so they could look out. Most of the water HAD gone. But they still waited for God to tell them to leave the ark.

And in a few weeks, God DID tell them.

What a day THAT was!

The great ark-door opened with a C-R-E-A-K. And out came Noah and his family.

And all the animals!

The animals acted all different ways. The brave ones, like the lions, made a dash for the forest. The timid ones, like the kittens, walked around in little circles, not quite sure what to do.

But Noah knew there was one thing HE wanted to do before he did anything else. He wanted to thank God. So the first thing he did was to gather some stones and pile them up and make an altar. And there Noah and his family knelt down and worshiped God and thanked him for saving them.

And God made Noah a VERY IMPORTANT promise. God said, "I will never again destroy the earth with a flood. And just so we'll remember, I will give you a sign. Every time it rains I'll put a rainbow in the sky. And when I see that rainbow I'll remember my promise."

And it turned out just as God had said. Every time it rained, sure enough, up in the sky was the most beautiful rainbow—just like a big curved bridge—shining with all its colors!

And Noah and his family were happy because God had kept them safe.

But most of all, God was pleased because Noah had remembered to thank him.

LET'S TALK ABOUT THE BIBLE STORY

Do you think you should be grateful to your parents? What about things they're supposed to do for you anyhow? It's their duty to take care of you and feed you. Do you think you should be thankful for that? It's YOUR duty to do chores and run errands and obey. But do you like to get thanked for doing these things? How do you think people feel when you thank them? How do they feel when you don't thank them? Do you really think it matters to God—whether or not you thank him?

A BIBLE VERSE TO LEARN

Oh give thanks to the LORD, for He is good. (Psalm 107:1, *NASB*)

LET'S TALK TO GOD

Dear God, it's easy to be thankful for special things, like

presents and trips and surprises. Help us to remember to be thankful for things we don't even notice, like air to breathe and water and our houses and things like that. And above all help us to be thankful for your loving care. In Jesus' name, Amen.

NOW FIND THIS STORY IN YOUR BIBLE
It's in Genesis 8:10–22 and 9:8–19.

STORY 7

THE STRANGE JOURNEY

Did you ever watch your mother knit mittens? They didn't look like mittens at first, did they? Just needles, clicking along, and just yarn, twisting in little loops—click-twist-loop, click-twist-LOOP. Ridiculous!

"How do you KNOW they're going to be mittens?" you ask.

"Oh I just KNOW," she says, with a very smug look. "I'm not worried. I'm following directions, a step at a time. And I know the DIRECTIONS are right." And you just have to believe her. She DOES seem to know what she's doing!

Once there was a man who followed God's directions. One step at a time. And he didn't worry either. Because he knew that God was his friend, and God's directions were RIGHT. This man's name was ABRAHAM, and he lived—oh, a long,

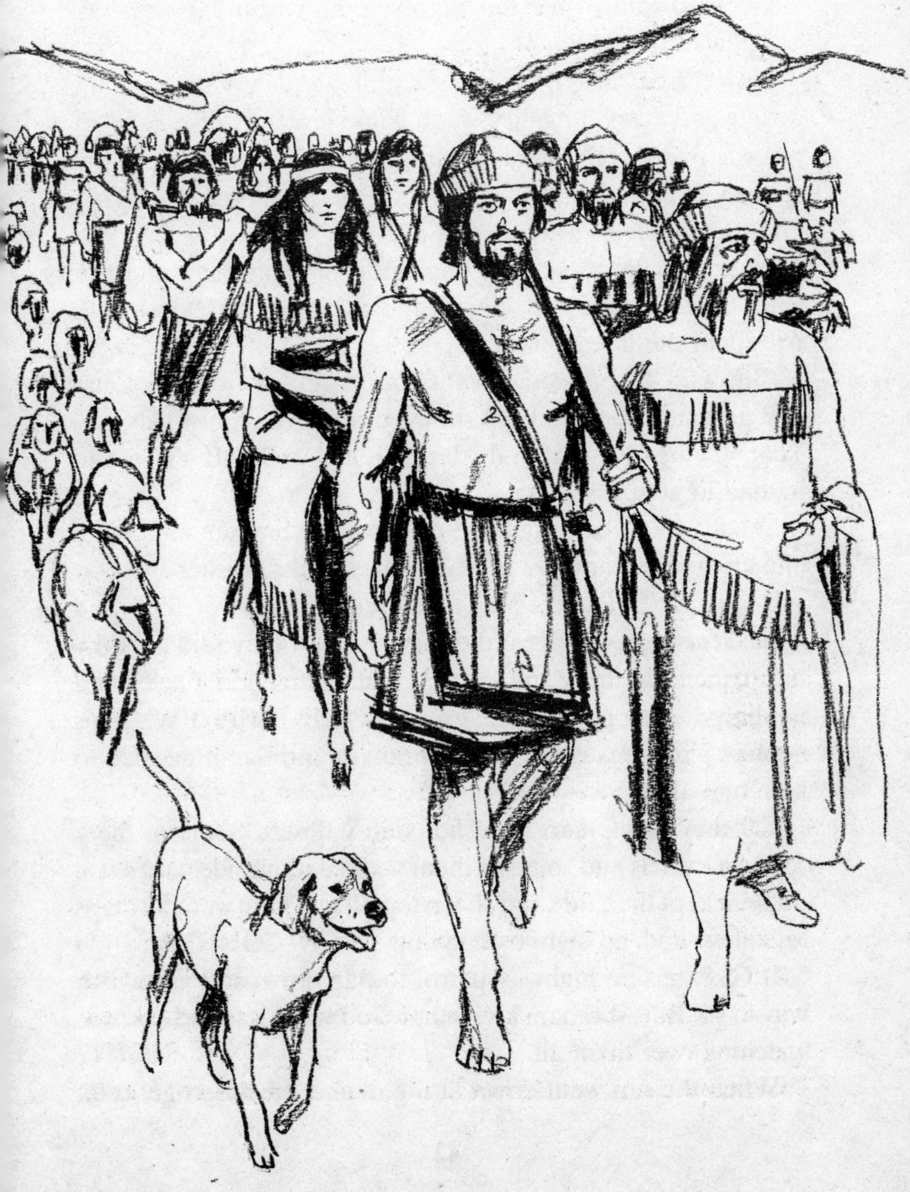

long time ago. He had a wife, and her name was Sarah. He had a family—brothers and cousins and nephews and nieces and uncles and aunts—just the biggest family you can imagine. They lived in the city of Ur.

Now the city of Ur was very beautiful and very rich, and the people had everything they wanted and it seemed like an ideal place to live. But there was one thing wrong. The people in this country did not love God. They didn't even pray to God. They prayed to images of wood and metal.

Abraham used to go out under the stars at night and talk with God. It was on one of those nights that God gave Abraham the directions.

God said, "Abraham, I want you to get out of this country and go to another land. I'll show you the way." Just like that. That was the first step. And Abraham had to BELIEVE it. And he had to get busy.

What a lot of packing there was to do! Abraham and Sarah and all their servants got to work. They packed dishes and pots and rugs and blankets and tents and all kinds of food and loaded them on camels and donkeys. Then they said good-by to all their brothers and cousins and aunts and uncles and nephews and nieces—all except ONE NEPHEW. This nephew's name was Lot, and Abraham and Sarah decided to take him along.

Off they went, across the hot sunny desert. Some of them rode on camels and some of them walked alongside, and some of them kept the cattle and sheep together. There were no maps to follow and no signposts saying "NEW COUNTRY—159 MILES," and no highway patrol to flag down and ask which way to go. But Abraham knew that God was his friend and was watching over them all.

When the sun went down at night, and the desert got cold,

they stopped and built a fire and got their supper, and put up their tents and unrolled their blankets. Before they went to bed, they thanked God for watching over them. And after they were all asleep, Abraham went out under the stars again and talked with God.

Abraham wasn't worried. He knew they were going to reach the new land. He knew, because he was following God, one step at a time, and God was his friend. And Abraham knew that the directions were RIGHT.

LET'S TALK ABOUT THE BIBLE STORY

Is it hard for you to follow directions when you don't know what you're doing and you just have to BELIEVE somebody? Should you believe just ANYBODY? It depends on who is giving the directions, doesn't it? You have to trust the person who is giving the directions. How can you show that you trust your parents? God?

A BIBLE VERSE TO LEARN

Abraham believed God, . . . and he was called the Friend of God. (James 2:23, *KJV*)

LET'S TALK TO GOD

Dear God, thank you for being the kind of a friend we can believe. When you give directions, we know that they are right. Thank you for giving us fathers and mothers we can trust. In Jesus' name, Amen.

NOW FIND THIS STORY IN YOUR BIBLE

It's in Genesis 12:1–9 and 13:1–4.

STORY 8

A SELFISH CHOICE

God was a real friend to Abraham. Just as he had promised, he watched over Abraham and the people who were with him, and showed them every step of the way to the new land. And the directions WERE right. For finally—

There it was!

Just as God had promised! And what a beautiful land it was. It was just like a picture—long, rolling hills covered with grass like a green velvet carpet, and trees and flowers. And all for Abraham and his family and Lot and his family to live in!

The first thing they all did was to pile stones up and make an altar. Then they knelt down and thanked God for keeping them safe. And then they unpacked their things and began to settle down to live.

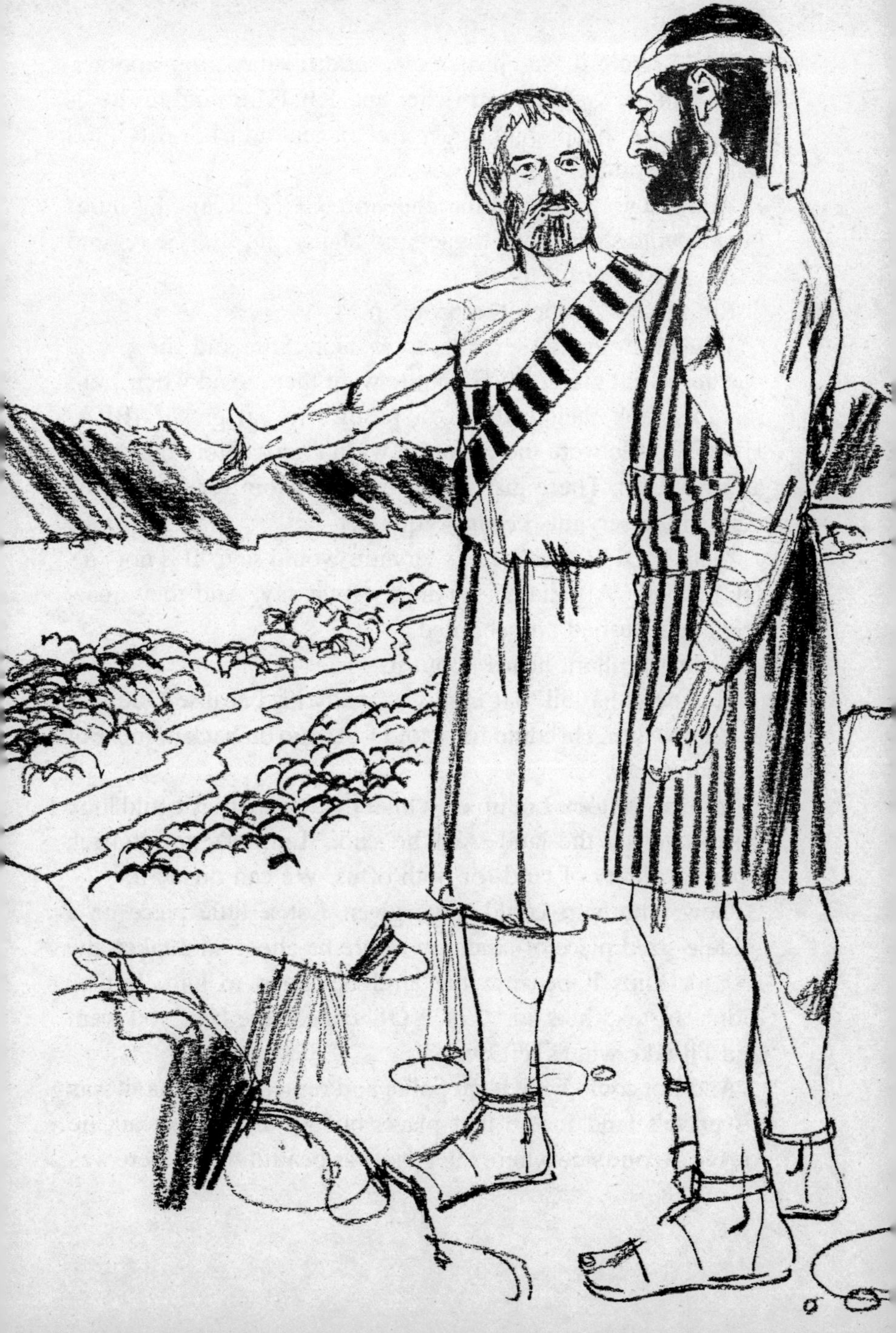

For a while it was just one wonderful day after another. Abraham grew richer and richer and RICHER, and his herds of cattle and sheep grew bigger and bigger and BIGGER—and that was wonderful.

And Lot grew richer and richer and RICHER, and his herds of cattle and sheep grew bigger and bigger and BIGGER—and that was wonderful too.

But there was one little problem.

When Abraham's servants took their cattle and sheep to a pasture to eat grass, LOT'S cattle were there. And when Lot's servants took their cattle to a pasture to eat grass, ABRAHAM'S cattle were there. And it wasn't long before they were all mixed up. There just wasn't enough room for everybody. And so the servants began to quarrel.

"This is OUR spot!" Lot's servants would say. "It is not—it's OUR spot!" Abraham's servants would say. And they quarreled and pushed and shouted.

Then Abraham heard about it.

He knew that all that land was really his because God had given it to him. He could have told Lot to go on back home. But he didn't.

Instead, he took Lot up on a high hill, where they could look down over all the land. And he said, "Lot, let's not quarrel. There is plenty of land for both of us. We can divide it."

Now Abraham could have given Lot a little piece or a middle-sized piece of land, anywhere he chose, and taken the rest for himself because the land belonged to him. But he didn't. Instead he said, "Lot, YOU choose the land you want and I'll take what's left over."

And Lot could have been polite and remembered that it was his uncle's land in the first place, but he didn't. Instead, he looked on one side where the grass was beautiful and there was a big river—and he looked on the OTHER side where there wasn't much grass and there was no river—and he pointed to the best side and said, "Uncle Abraham, I'll take THAT side."

And he did.

He took his family and his servants and his cattle and his sheep and moved down into the very best part of the land, and settled down to live. Abraham and Sarah and their servants, and all their cattle and sheep stayed in the hills. And Abraham built another altar and thanked God for being his friend.

Abraham wasn't worried. He knew that he didn't have the best piece of land—but he knew that he had done the right thing.

And doing the right thing was what counted—with God.

LET'S TALK ABOUT THE BIBLE STORY

What is the first thing Abraham did when he reached the new land? What other ways could Abraham and Lot have settled their quarrel? Do you think Abraham did the right thing? Why? He was left with the worst piece of land; why wasn't he worried?

A BIBLE VERSE TO LEARN

Treat others as you want them to treat you. (Luke 6:13, *TLB*)

LET'S TALK TO GOD

Dear God, it isn't very easy to choose the next best and give somebody else the best. But we know that being polite and doing the right thing is what counts with you. Help us to want to please you. In Jesus' name, Amen.

NOW FIND THIS STORY IN YOUR BIBLE

It's in Genesis 13:5–18.

STORY 9

THE VISITORS WHO MADE A PROMISE

Well, Abraham might have been left with the poorest piece of land, but God had not forgotten him. Abraham grew richer and richer and RICHER. His herds of sheep and cattle and camels and donkeys grew bigger and bigger and BIGGER. And as if that weren't enough, God made Abraham a very important promise. God promised Abraham he would have so many children, they would be harder to count than the grains of sand on the seashore.

Now Abraham and Sarah wanted children more than anything else in the world. And they knew God would keep His promise all right. There was only one little problem. God said SOME DAY—

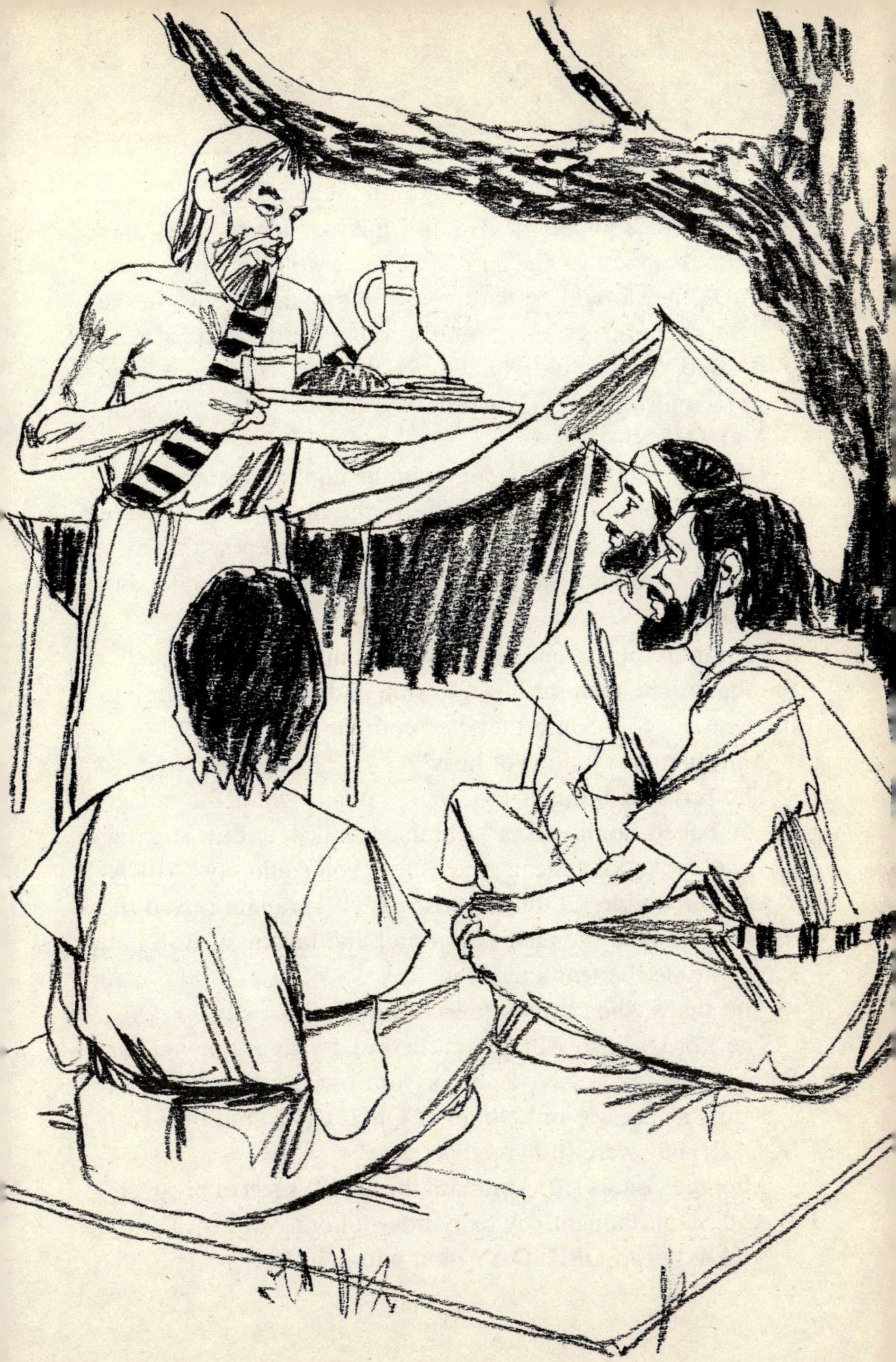

But He didn't say WHEN.

Well, the years went by and Abraham and Sarah got to be middle-aged, and they still didn't have children. God even spoke to Abraham again, and told him he would have so many children, they would be harder to count than the stars in the sky. But more years went by, and Abraham and Sarah got to be OLD, and they still didn't have any children. And more years went by and MORE years went by—

And THEN!

One day, Abraham was sitting in the door of his tent, when he looked up and saw three men in the distance. They were coming right toward his tent. Abraham didn't know that they were the Lord and two angels, for they looked just like any other men.

He ran to meet them and invited them to come and rest in the shade. The men sat down to rest, and Abraham went into the tent and told Sarah they had company.

And then everybody got busy!

The servants brought the men water to wash for dinner. Sarah baked some cakes. Abraham killed a calf and the servants cooked the meat. And before you could say "ABRAHAM"—a wonderful dinner was ready! Abraham served the dinner, and then the men sat around and talked, while Sarah stayed inside the tent and listened.

And that's when the wonderful thing happened.

The Lord said to Abraham, "Before a year is up, you and Sarah are going to have a son of your own, a baby boy."

Before a year was up! Not just SOME DAY—but PRETTY SOON! They were so happy!

After the visitors left, Abraham thought, "A son of my own."

And Sarah thought, "A baby boy—all our own!"

And not just SOME DAY—but within a year!

And sure enough, it was true.

God kept his promise, and before a year was up, Abraham and Sarah had a real live "squirgling" baby boy. He was fat and dimpled and beautiful.

The very first thing they did was to thank God for him. They named him "Isaac," and that means "laughter."

At first Isaac, couldn't do much of anything. And then he learned to smile, and then he learned to wiggle his toes, and then he learned how to put his foot in his mouth, and then he learned how to creep, and then he learned how to WALK.

And Abraham and Sarah kept thanking God for him. God had made a promise. And it had taken a long, long time. But he had kept it.

LET'S TALK ABOUT THE BIBLE STORY

Do you think every promise should be kept right away? Why not? Is it hard for you to wait for a "some day" promise? Do you think Abraham and Sarah believed God was doing right to make them wait? How do you know God will always keep His promises?

A BIBLE VERSE TO LEARN

God is faithful. (1 Corinthians 1:9, *KJV*)

LET'S TALK TO GOD

Dear God, we thank you that you ALWAYS keep your promises. Help us to be patient when we have to wait. And help us to be grateful. In Jesus' name, Amen.

NOW FIND THIS STORY IN YOUR BIBLE

It's in Genesis 13:14-18 and 15:1-16 and 18:1-10 and 21:1-7.

STORY 10

THE MAN WHO OBEYED GOD NO MATTER WHAT

Isaac grew and GREW. He grew to be a little boy, and it was time for him to run and play. He grew to be a big boy, and it was time for him to watch the sheep and to hunt. And was he ever HAPPY!

Why, Isaac meant laughter. And the days were filled with laughter indeed. Laughter and joy.

And while Isaac was running and playing and watching sheep and hunting, he was growing bigger and BIGGER.

Five years went by. Ten years went by.

Eleven years. TWELVE years!

Isaac was twelve years old!

And what a strapping healthy boy he was! He was lean and hard and chock-full of muscles, and brown from the sun. He could run fast, jump high, shoot an arrow straight, skip stones

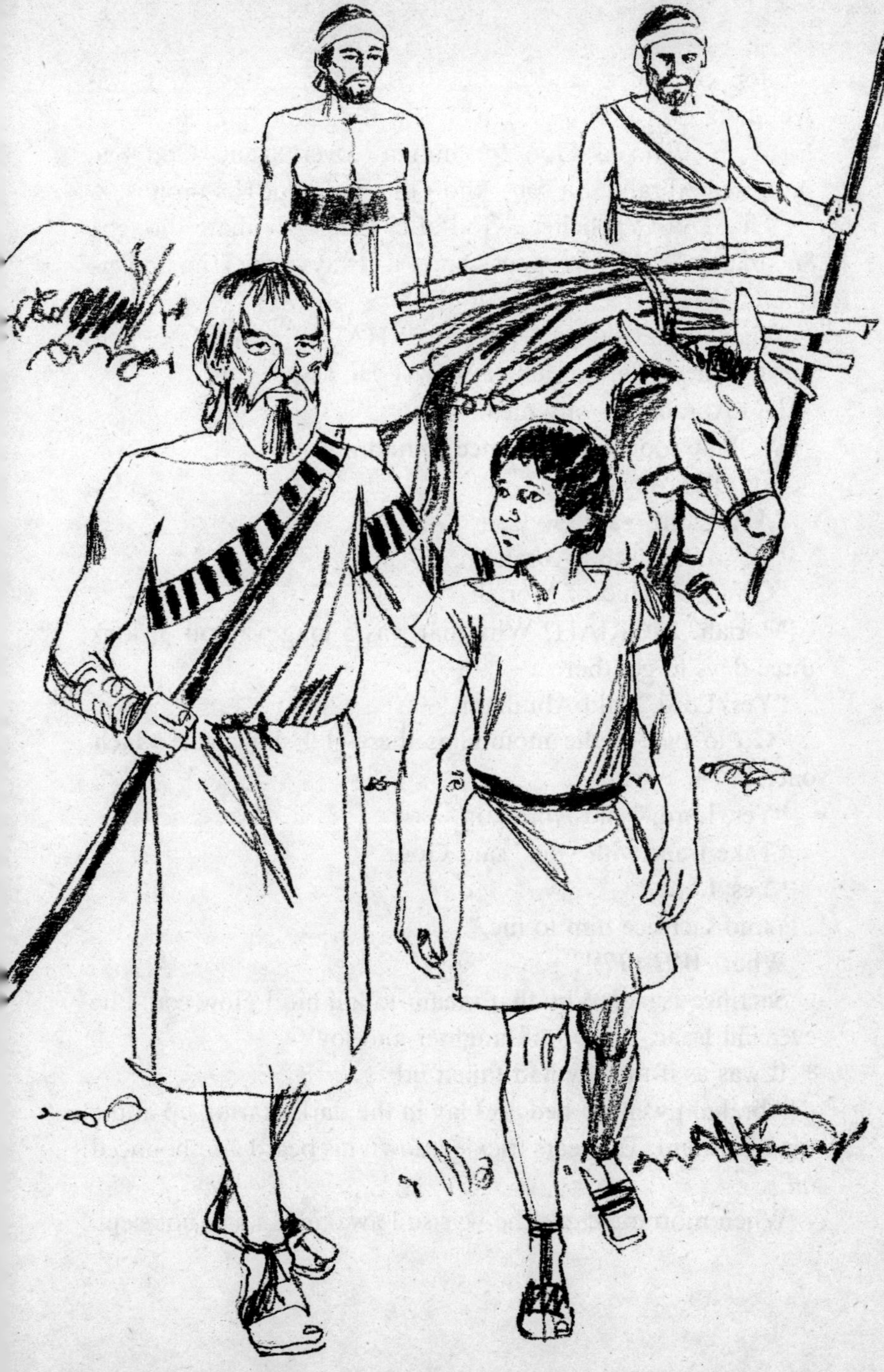

on top of water, and a hundred other things. And was Abraham ever proud of him! Every time Abraham looked at Isaac, he thanked God for him all over again. God had promised Abraham a son. And God had kept His promise.

"I'll ALWAYS believe God after this," Abraham thought, "no matter WHAT happens. And I'll always obey Him, too, no matter WHAT He asks me to do!"

What? Believe God no matter WHAT happens?

And obey Him no matter WHAT He asks?

Did Abraham really mean that?

Well, he soon had a chance to find out.

For ONE day—

"Abraham!" said God.

"Yes, Lord," said Abraham.

"Go to the land of Moriah—"

Moriah? MORIAH? Why that was a long way off. It took three days to get there.

"Yes, Lord," said Abraham.

"Go to one of the mountains there—I'll show you which one—"

"Yes, Lord," said Abraham.

"Take Isaac with you," said God.

"Yes, Lord."

"And sacrifice him to me."

What? *WHAT*?!!?

Sacrifice Isaac? Why that meant to kill him! How could he ever kill Isaac, his son of laughter and joy!

It was as if the sky had fallen in!

Abraham went to bed and lay in the dark, staring up at the top of his tent. The tears trickled down his beard and bounced off.

When morning came, he was still awake. He had not slept,

not one WINK—all night. He got up, and gathered all the things he needed for the journey to the mountains. He chopped wood to carry with them so they could build a fire for the sacrifice. He got the food they would need, and the water. And he loaded everything on a donkey. By that time, the others were awake. He called two servants to go along with him.

And then he called Isaac.

It was the HARDEST thing he'd ever had to do!

"We're going to a mountain in the land of Moriah," he said, "to worship God and offer him a sacrifice."

Abraham had decided to obey God, no matter WHAT!

"Everything is ready," he said. "Let's get started."

And they DID!

LET'S TALK ABOUT THE BIBLE STORY

Abraham believed God would make everything come out all right, no matter HOW bad things looked. What do YOU think? Do you think that was a hard test for Abraham? And what do you think he did? You'll find out in the next story!

A BIBLE VERSE TO LEARN

We ought to obey God. (Acts 5:29, *KJV*)

LET'S TALK TO GOD

Dear God, sometimes it's hard to obey you when we don't know what you're up to. Help us to believe you, even when we don't know what's going to happen next. In Jesus' name, Amen.

NOW FIND THIS STORY IN YOUR BIBLE

It's in Genesis 22:1-3.

STORY 11

THE HARDEST TEST IN THE WORLD

Abraham and Isaac and the servants started out on their journey to Moriah.

It was a long journey. One day went by. And Abraham thought, "I WILL obey God."

Two days went by. And Abraham thought, "No matter WHAT."

Three days went by. And Abraham thought, "I KNOW God will make everything come out all right. I WILL believe Him."

And then they reached the mountain.

"Stay here with the donkey," Abraham told the servants. "Isaac and I will go up the mountain and worship. And he—HUP!—hiked the wood for the fire up on Isaac's strong young shoulders.

And so they started up the mountain, Abraham and Isaac, his son of laughter and joy.

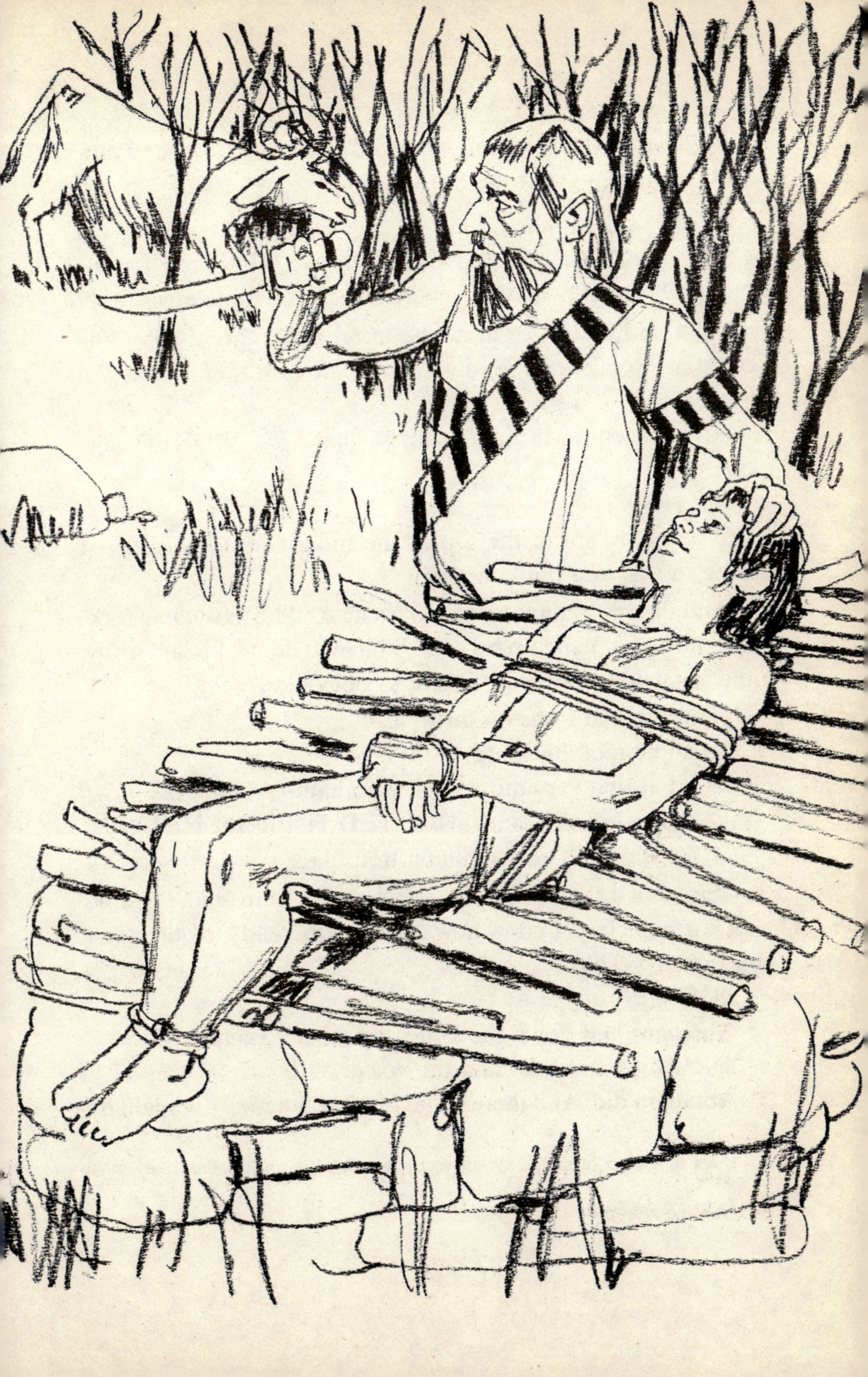

"Do we have everything we need?" said Isaac. "The knife, and the flint* to start the fire?"

"Yes," said Abraham.

And then Isaac stopped in his tracks. "The lamb for the sacrifice!" he said. "Father, where is the lamb for the sacrifice?"

Abraham had to swallow the lump in his throat before he could answer. Then, "God will take care of it, son," he said at last.

And somehow, Abraham knew that God WOULD take care of it.

But HOW?

When they got to the top of the mountain, they gathered some stones, and built an altar.

And then Abraham turned to Isaac. And he took some rope. And he began to tie up his son. "I have to do it," he said softly, and his voice trembled. "I have to obey God."

And he laid Isaac on the altar—

And he took his knife—

And at that very moment—"Abraham—Abraham!"

An angel of the Lord SHOUTED IT FROM HEAVEN!

"Yes, Lord," said Abraham, trembling.

"Lay down the knife," the angel of the Lord said, "and do not harm the boy. I know now that you are ready to obey me—no matter WHAT."

PHEW!!!!!

Abraham laid down the knife and untied Isaac.

"Now turn around," said the voice.

Abraham did. And there behind him was a ram** caught by

---

*Flint is a kind of stone. When you rub two of them together, they make SPARKS.

**A male sheep.

its horns in a bush! God had taken care of the sacrifice. It was right there, before Abraham's eyes!

He killed the ram and put it on the altar and built a fire. And the tears trickled down his beard and bounced off. But this time they were tears of joy! God had not wanted him to kill his son after all! God was only testing him, to see if he would obey, NO MATTER WHAT. And Abraham had passed the test!

Abraham and Isaac HUGGED each other. (The father who obeyed God, and the son whose name meant laughter and joy.) And they went back down the mountain and started for home.

God HAD made everything come out all right!

LET'S TALK ABOUT THE BIBLE STORY

God did not really want Abraham to kill his son. It was only a test. Abraham believed that God would make everything come out all right, no matter how bad things looked. God expects us to obey him no matter what he asks us to do. But always remember, God would NEVER test anyone else the way he tested Abraham that day.

A BIBLE VERSE TO LEARN

We ought to obey God. (Acts 5:29, *KJV*)

LET'S TALK TO GOD

Dear God, we know you would never give us a test like Abraham's. Help us to always obey you, no matter WHAT. And thank you for always making everything come out all right.

NOW FIND THIS STORY IN YOUR BIBLE

It's in Genesis 22:4–14.

STORY 12

How a Prayer Was Answered

Isaac was still alive!
Indeed he was!
Oh, joy!
He grew and grew and GREW—

And before you could say "Abraham and Sarah"—(or so it seemed)—he grew to be a man and it was time for him to be married. So Abraham told his servant Eliezer to go back to the country where Abraham's relatives lived and find Isaac a wife.

"Don't find just ANY wife, Eliezer," said Abraham. "Find just the RIGHT wife. Ask God to give you directions. And find a wife who is kind."

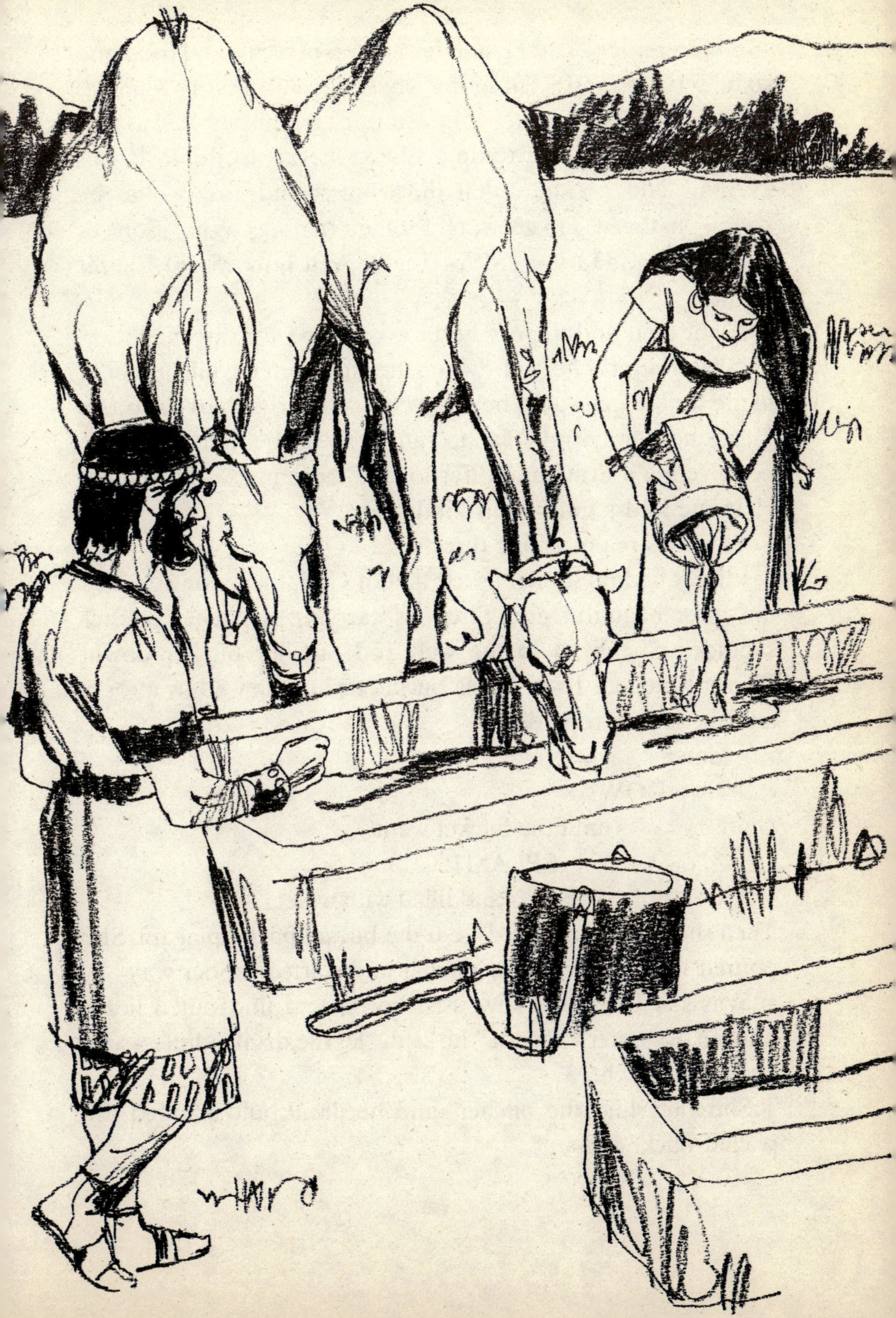

So Eliezer took camels and jewels and presents and food and some servants and went to the city where Abraham's relatives lived. When they got there, they stopped by the city well to rest. And while they were resting, Eliezer began to think. It was evening, and he knew that the women and girls would be coming to the well to get water for their families. What if one of THEM was the right girl for Isaac? And how would Eliezer know?

Right then and there, Eliezer asked God for directions.

"Please, God," he said, "when the girls from the village come to the well to get water, help me choose the right girl for Isaac. I'll ask her for a drink of water, and if she is the right one, have her give me a drink and offer to give the camels a drink, too. Help me find a girl who is kind."

That was really asking directions!

Eliezer had no sooner asked that of God, then along came—the most beautiful girl! She was carrying a pitcher on her shoulder. She went to the well and put her pitcher down. Eliezer watched. There was a bucket tied to the well by a rope, and she let the rope down—

down—

DOWN—

until the bucket went

SPLASH!—

and filled with water.

Then she pulled and p-u-l-l-e-d the bucket back up again. She poured the water into her pitcher and started on her way.

Was she the one? Now was the time to find out! Eliezer hurried up to her. "Please," he said, "let me drink a little water from your pitcher."

She gave him the pitcher—and he drank and handed the pitcher back, and—

"I'll draw water for your camels, also," she said.

Well, when you stop to think that one camel drinks about twenty gallons of water when he's thirsty, and that Eliezer had ten camels with him, and you multiply twenty by ten, you can see that this girl wasn't just kind. She was EXTRA kind. Two hundred gallons of water! She was the one!

Eliezer watcher her while she drew water and more water and MORE water for the camels. And he bowed his head then and there to thank God for giving him directions, and for choosing such a kind and polite girl for Isaac's wife. Then he gave her some rings and bracelets.

"Whose daughter are you?" he said. "Is there room for us to stay in your father's house?"

She told him her name was Rebekah, and there was LOTS of room for them in her father's house.

And when Eliezer went to her father's house and told her father and mother that God had chosen Rebekah for Isaac's wife, they let her go back with him!

And that's how it happened, that when Eliezer went back to Abraham, he had a wife for Isaac. Not just ANY wife. But the RIGHT wife. She was extra kind. God had certainly given Eliezer the right directions!

LET'S TALK ABOUT THE BIBLE STORY

Is it a good idea to ask God for directions when you're about to do something important? How about something that doesn't seem very important? Do you suppose everything you do is important to God? Do you think Eliezer was wise to ask God for directions? Do you think Rebekah was foolish to be so extra kind? Isn't it good enough to just do want you are asked to do? Is it dumb to do something extra? Do you suppose God wants you to? What do you think?

A BIBLE VERSE TO LEARN
Even a child is known by his doings, whether his work be pure, and whether it be right. (Proverbs 20:11, *KJV*)

LET'S TALK TO GOD
Dear God, we thank you that you are interested in everything we do—both the BIG things and the LITTLE things. And we know that it's good to be kind. But it's better to be EXTRA kind whenever we can. In Jesus' name, Amen.

NOW FIND THIS STORY IN YOUR BIBLE
It's in Genesis 24:1–67.

STORY 13

THE MAN WHO RAN AWAY

Well, Isaac and Rebekah got married, and God was good to them. He gave them—not ONE baby—but TWO babies, born at the same time. They were TWINS and their names were Esau and Jacob.

God was good to Esau and Jacob, too. They had a good father and mother. They had lots of things to do. They could play together and make bows and arrows and hunt.

But one thing was wrong.

They couldn't get along together. They quarreled and pushed and kicked.

When they grew up to be men, God was still good to them. They had everything—sheep and cattle and gold and silver. They could work together and make bows and arrows and hunt.

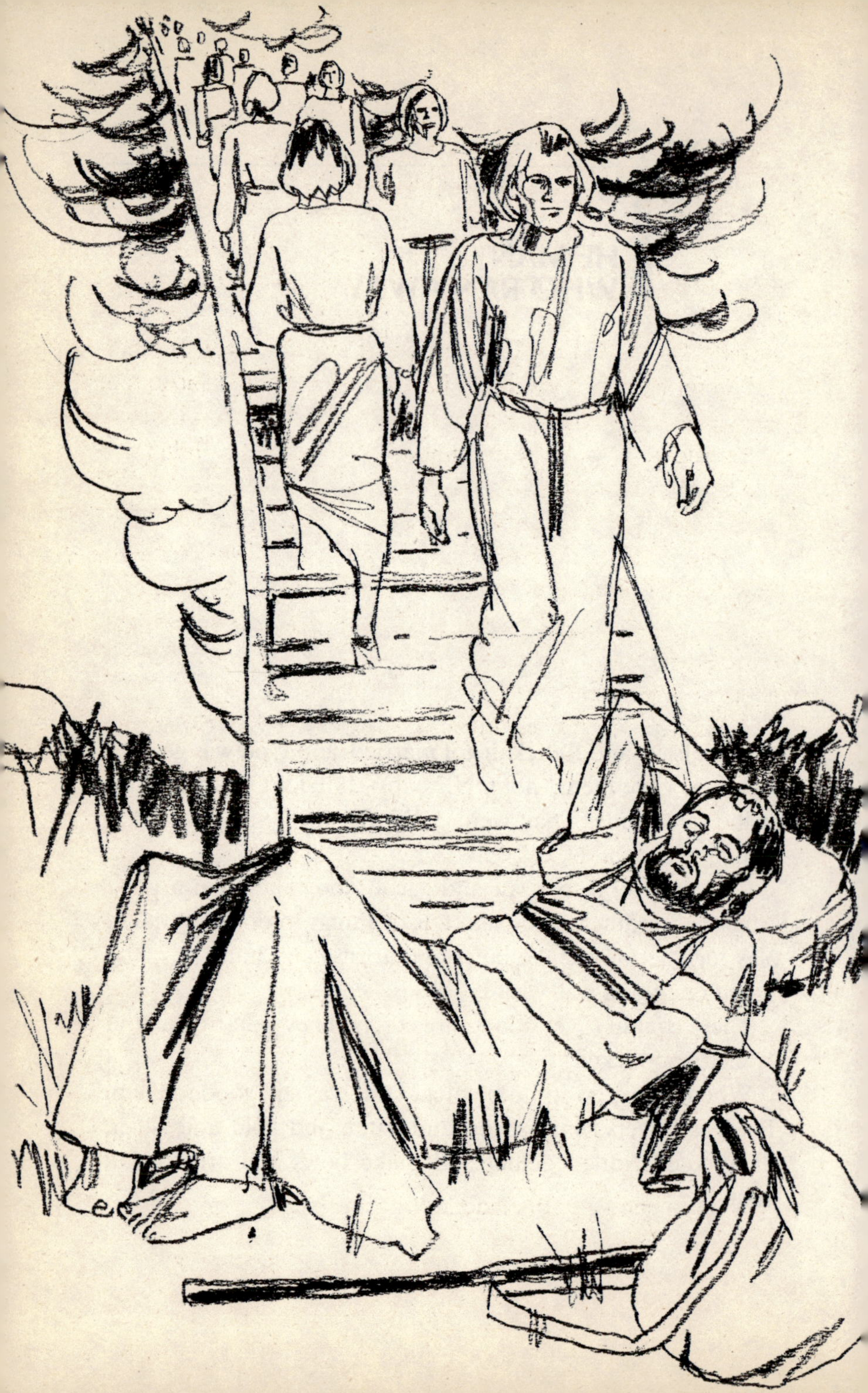

But the same thing was still wrong.

They couldn't get along together. They quarreled and lied and cheated.

One day, Jacob cheated his brother Esau—and Esau was SO angry that Jacob was afraid. His mother, Rebekah, was afraid, too. "You'd better go away before Esau hurts you," she told Jacob. "Go back to my country and stay with my brother Laban for awhile." And that's how it happened that Jacob ran away.

He said good-by to his mother and father. But he didn't say good-by to Esau.

He was afraid of Esau.

Jacob ran away without camels. Without servants. Without friends. He hurried through the stony paths of the hill country. He walked across the fields of the flat country. And he sneaked through the mountain passes. And wondered every minute if Esau was following!

As the sun went down, every shadow looked like Esau. And when it got dark, every noise sounded like Esau. Jacob curled up on the ground and put his head on a stone. He felt as if NOBODY cared what happened to him. "Nobody is with me," he thought. And then he fell asleep. He was sleeping soundly,
when—

suddenly—
there was a great big ladder, right before Jacob's eyes! It started at the ground and reached all the way up to the sky. And there were angels going up and coming down. And he heard the voice of God saying, "I am with you—and I will watch over you wherever you go."

It was a dream! Why, Jacob wasn't alone—GOD was with him!

Then suddenly the ladder was gone—

and the angels were gone—
and God's voice was gone—
and Jacob awoke.

But he didn't feel alone any more. And he didn't feel afraid any more. He took the stone he had used for a pillow, and set it up for an altar, and thanked God for watching over him. And he started on his way again—

Without camels. Without servants. Without friends.

But God was with him. And he knew he'd be all right. He knew he'd get to his Uncle Laban's house safely.

And he did!

LET'S TALK ABOUT THE BIBLE STORY

Well, Jacob had certainly disobeyed God. He quarreled and he lied and he cheated. But STILL God said, "I am with you—and I will watch over you wherever you go." Did that give Jacob an excuse for disobeying God? What do you think?

A BIBLE VERSE TO LEARN

I am with you, and will keep you wherever you go. (Genesis 28:15, *NASB*)

LET'S TALK TO GOD

Dear God, we know that you are still with us, even when we disobey you. But we know that that is no EXCUSE for disobeying. Please help us to OBEY you. And thank you for being with us always. In Jesus' name, Amen.

NOW FIND THIS STORY IN YOUR BIBLE

It's in Genesis 27:41–45 and 28:10–22.

STORY 14

TWO BROTHERS IN TROUBLE

Jacob went to live with his Uncle Laban, and got married and started a cattle business of his own. And then—his family grew and grew until he had eleven children and many servants. And his business grew until he had cattle and sheep by the thousands.

The weeks went by and the months went by, until TWENTY YEARS had gone by—and Jacob had almost everything in the world he wanted.

Except for one thing.

Jacob wanted to go back home. He thought about it and thought about it. And then—one day God told him he COULD go back to his own country again—and God said, "I will be with you."

A trip back home! Just imagine that!

Jacob and his family and servants packed their things and started out—with camels and donkeys and sheep and cattle and

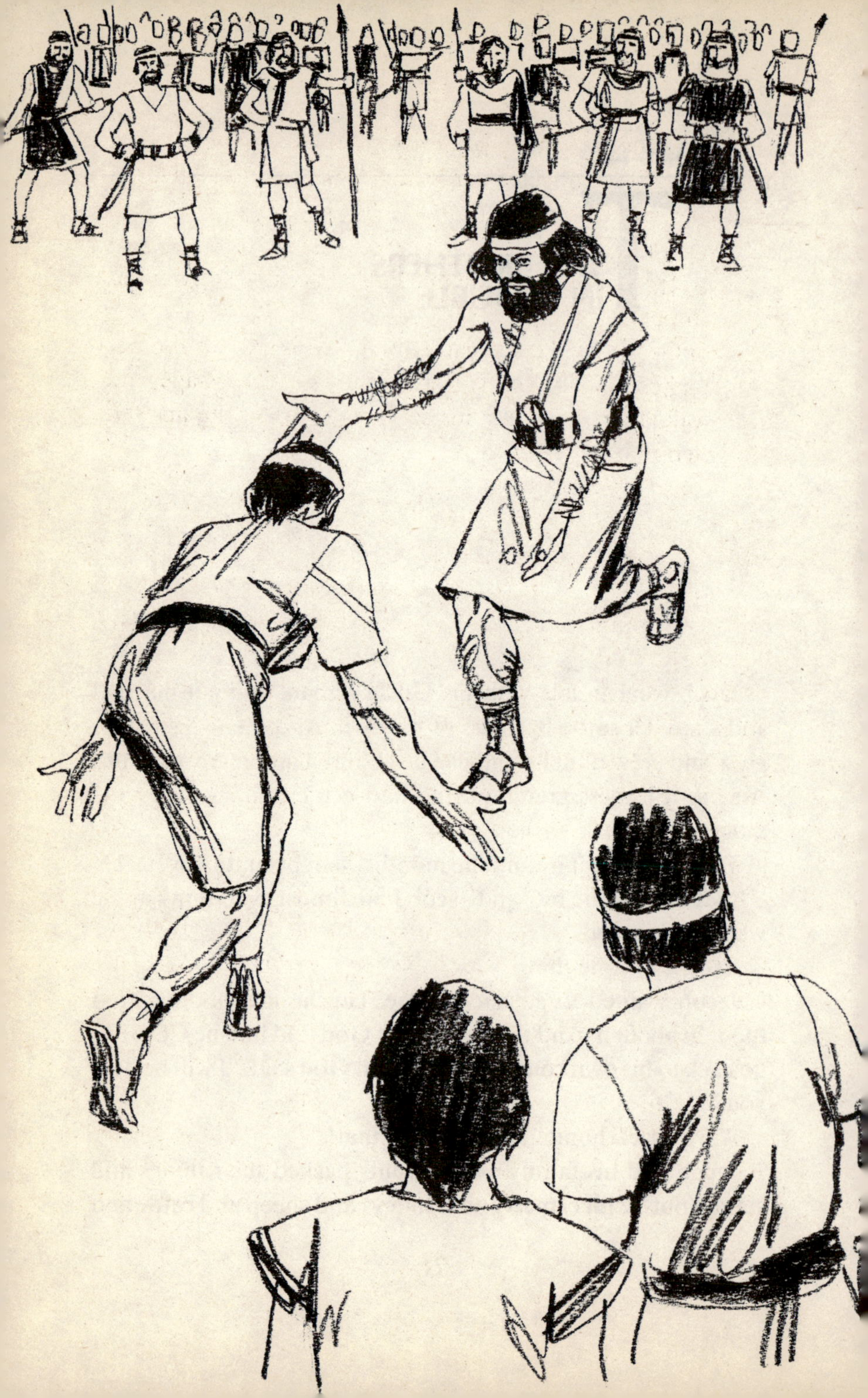

just about everything they could carry. What a cloud of dust they made as they traveled across the desert! Jacob thought of his mother and father and Esau—

ESAU!

Would Esau still want to kill him? Jacob became more afraid by the minute.

He sent some servants ahead with a message to his brother Esau that he was on the way. It was a very polite message, and Jacob waited anxiously for his servants to bring the answer. And when the answer came—

It wasn't polite—

It wasn't IMpolite—

It was FRIGHTENING!

It said that Esau was coming to meet Jacob—with 400 men! What did it mean? Jacob didn't know. But it was time for him to get busy.

First he divided his family and servants and cattle into two groups, so if Esau killed one group there would still be some left. Then he knelt down and asked God to help him. And then he sent servants ahead with a gift for Esau. A BIG gift. Hundreds of goats and sheep and camels and cows and donkeys.

And then both groups traveled on.

While they traveled, Jacob thought, "Esau—Esau—Esau—." And the clop-clop of the camels' feet seemed to say, "Eee—sau, Eee—sau, Eee—sau"—until suddenly

there off in the distance—

Esau was coming!

Esau came closer and closer and CLOSER—

And Jacob could stand it no longer. He ran ahead of his servants and his cattle and his family. He ran toward Esau. Then he bowed to the ground. And he ran and he bowed and he ran and he bowed, until he had bowed seven times. And Esau ran toward Jacob—and he put his arms around Jacob's neck—and kissed him!

It was all over—the quarreling and hating and cheating. Esau forgave his brother and they made up, right then and there. And then they all went back home together.

Now Jacob could be COMPLETELY happy. He had his family—he was going home—and his brother Esau had forgiven him. That was something to thank God for.

And Jacob did!

LET'S TALK ABOUT THE BIBLE STORY

Jacob was afraid of Esau; does that make him a coward? Do you think it is all right to be afraid? It depends on the REASON, doesn't it? Do you think Jacob had good reason? Why do you think it took real courage for Jacob to run toward Esau? Esau had every reason to stay angry with Jacob, but he forgave him. What should you do when someone wants to make up with you? What can you do when it is hard to forgive someone?

A BIBLE VERSE TO LEARN

Be kind to one another, tender-hearted, forgiving each other. (Ephesians 4:32, *NASB*)

LET'S TALK TO GOD

Dear God, help us to remember that it is not a sin to be afraid. The important thing is to do what's right whether we're afraid or not. Help us to forgive when other people want to make up. It IS a sin to stay angry. Thank you, God, for watching over us, when we're afraid, and when we are not. In Jesus' name, Amen.

NOW FIND THIS STORY IN YOUR BIBLE
It's in Genesis 31:3 and 32:1-21 and 33:1-20.

For Us All

Sing in a question and answer dialogue as indicated in the song.

(Leader) Who made the trees and the birds and flow'rs? *(Children)* God made the trees and the birds and flow'rs! *(Leader)* Who made the sea? *(Children)* God made the sea! *(Leader)* Who made the sky? *(Children)* God made the sky! *(Leader)* Who made you and me? *(Children)* God made you and me! *(Leader)* Thank you, God, *(Children)* Thank you God, Thank you, God, Thank you, God. *Softly*

Words and Music: James A. Ruth.
© Copyright 1976 G/L Publications. Used by permission.

75

PART TWO
STORIES OF JOSEPH

STORY 15

THE GIFT THAT CAUSED TROUBLE

Now ordinarily a gift is a very jolly thing. You open it and you are jolly and you thank the one who gave it to you and he is jolly and you show it to your friends and they are jolly and there you have it; nothing but fun and happiness. Everybody knows that. But the gift in this story was NOT ordinary. This gift brought nothing but trouble—to a boy named Joseph.

Joseph lived way back in Bible times, and he was the happiest, bubbliest boy you could ever imagine. He was tall and strong, and he could leap over a wall or scramble through the bushes faster than the best of them. He had ten BIG brothers and one baby brother, and when they all sat around the breakfast table and passed the barley cakes and honey, there was always plenty of excitement.

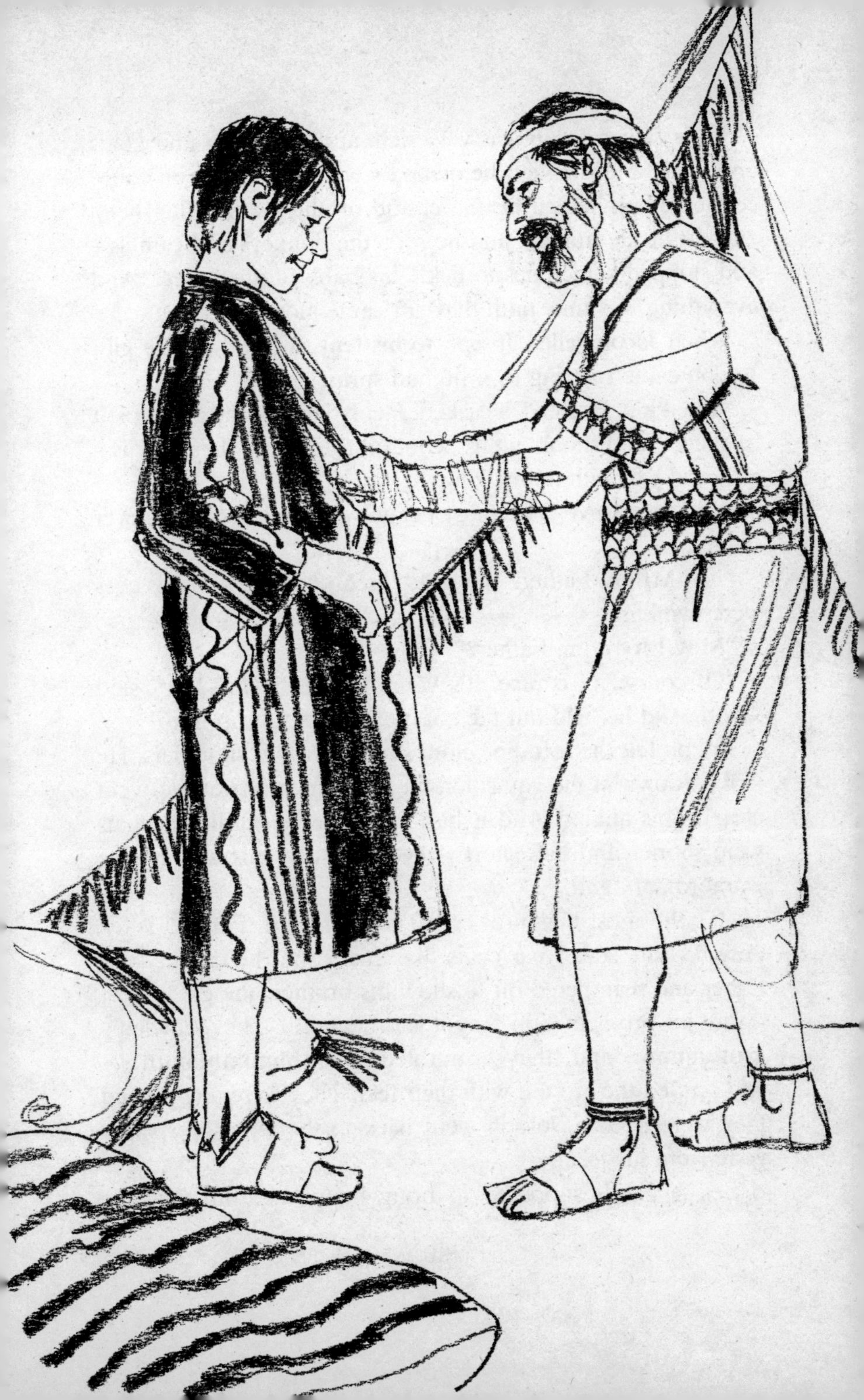

Their father Jacob was very rich, and the sheep and goats and cattle and donkeys he owned were more than you could count. Joseph helped his father and brothers watch the sheep and cattle. He hunted, and he rode the donkeys and camels—and stopped sometimes to tickle his baby brother's feet. And everything was fine, until that gift came along.

When Jacob called Joseph to his tent to give him the gift, Joseph came running as if he had springs in his feet.

"What is it, Father?" he asked. Jacob held out the gift, took it by the top and shook out its beautiful folds—and there it was—splashed gay with many colors.

It was a COAT. The most beautiful coat Joseph had ever seen!

"Is it MINE, Father?" he cried. Jacob nodded yes. His eyes were twinkling.

"May I try it on, Father?"

"Of course, of course. It's yours to KEEP, my son," said Jacob. And he held out the coat for Joseph to slip into.

Joseph felt the soft, fine cloth slither over his shoulders. He looked down at the gay colors in amazement. The coat went clear to his ankles! And it had long sleeves! Ordinary coats were shorter and had short sleeves. Clearly, this was a most extraordinary gift!

"It's the most beautiful coat I've ever seen, Father! Why, only favorite sons wear coats like this!" And he thanked his father and scampered off to show his brothers the gift.

But his brothers didn't say it was beautiful. They scowled—hrummmmf—and they mumbled—mumblmumblmumbl—and scuffed the ground with their feet. They were angry. And they were jealous. Joseph went back to the tent, the springs gone from his feet.

Yes—a gift is supposed to bring happiness. But this one

brought nothing but trouble. Trouble to a boy named Joseph and to his whole family. Because Joseph's brothers were jealous.

But Joseph knew that God was watching over him and that God would take care of him. And God did.

LET'S TALK ABOUT THE BIBLE STORY

What makes people jealous? Do you think Joseph's brothers had good reason to be jealous? After all, they WERE older; perhaps one of them should have gotten the coat. Even if we have a REASON to be jealous—what does God want us to do?

A BIBLE VERSE TO LEARN

Jesus said, This I command you, that you love one another. (John 15:17, *NASB*)

LET'S TALK TO GOD

Dear God, help us to be GLAD when somebody else gets a gift, even if it's something we wanted ourselves. And even if we have a good REASON to be jealous help us not to be. We thank you for all the good things you give us. In Jesus' name, Amen.

NOW FIND THIS STORY IN YOUR BIBLE

It's in Genesis 37:1-4.

STORY 16

THE DREAMS THAT CAUSED TROUBLE

Joseph had everything that a boy could want. But there was one thing wrong. His brothers were jealous. They were jealous because their father Jacob loved Joseph the best. They were jealous because Jacob gave Joseph a beautiful coat. And, as if that weren't enough, two OTHER things happened to make them jealous! Two dreams! and Joseph dreamed them.

The first dream was a strange one. Joseph probably told his brothers about it at breakfast.

"Know what?" said Joseph. "I had the most amazing dream last night." And he reached for the barley cakes. "In my dream, we were all tying grain up in bundles. And MY bundle stood up straight. But YOUR bundles—" He asked for the honey. His brothers watched him.

"And our bundles? What did our bundles do?" they asked.

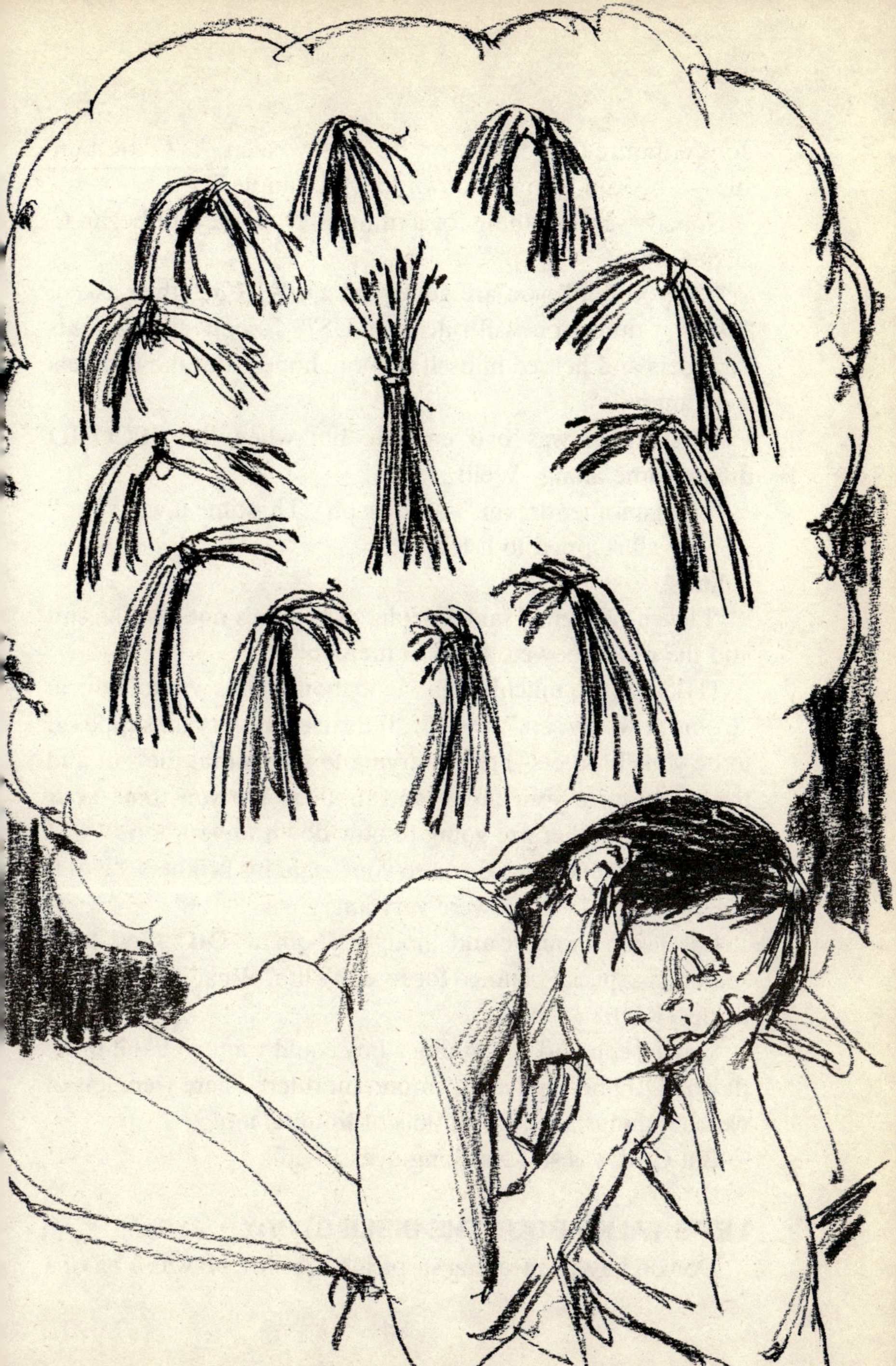

Joseph poured his honey on his barley cakes. "YOUR bundles—" he said, "bowed down to MY bundle."

Nobody said anything for a minute. Then they all began to talk at once.

"Do you think you are going to be a KING?" they asked. "Do you think you will rule over US?" Joseph shrugged his shoulders and helped himself to more honey. But the brothers were angry.

That dream was bad enough, but when the SECOND dream came along—Well!

"I had another dream," said Joseph. "This time it was stars."

They all stopped to listen.

Stars!

"Eleven of them," said Joseph. "And that's not all. The sun and the moon bowed down to me, too!"

THIS was too much! Even Jacob thought this was too much. "Come now, my son," he said. "If the eleven stars are supposed to be your brothers—are you trying to tell us that the sun and the moon were your father and mother? Do you think your father and mother are going to bow down to you, too?"

"WE'LL never bow down to you!" said his brothers. "Not if we can help it!" They were very angry.

But Jacob thought and thought about it. DID God have something special planned for Joseph's life? What if that dream came TRUE?

Yes, Joseph had everything a boy could want. What if some day he DID become a big, important ruler? There were lots of exciting things ahead. And lots of trouble, too!

But God was still watching over Joseph.

LET'S TALK ABOUT THE BIBLE STORY

Do you have a sneaking suspicion that Joseph was a bit of a

show-off? How else could he have acted over the dreams? This time even Joseph's FATHER was upset. Why do you think he had reason to be? What sort of plan do you think God had in store for Joseph?

A BIBLE VERSE TO LEARN

Love your neighbor as much as you love yourself. (Matthew 22:39, *TLB*)

LET'S TALK TO GOD

Dear God, help us not to be jealous, even when we know somebody else is going to be boss over us and we think he has no right to be. Help us to remember that YOU plan all these things, and that when we obey others, like kids who are safety patrolmen and monitors in school, we are really obeying YOU. In Jesus' name, Amen.

NOW FIND THIS STORY IN YOUR BIBLE

It's in Genesis 37:5–11.

STORY 17

THE ERRAND THAT ENDED IN TROUBLE

Joseph's brothers hated him.

"Dreamer!" they said, whenever he walked past.

"Good-by, 'Dreamer'!" they laughed when they went off to another part of the country to find new pastures for the sheep and cattle.

After they were gone, Joseph didn't have any more dreams. And as the weeks went by, he forgot about trouble.

And then, one day, Jacob gave Joseph a very important errand to do.

"My son," said Jacob, "I want you to find your brothers and bring me back news that they are safe."

Go find his brothers! Why they were in Shechem—at least 60 miles away! It would mean walking all day and sleeping out at night—

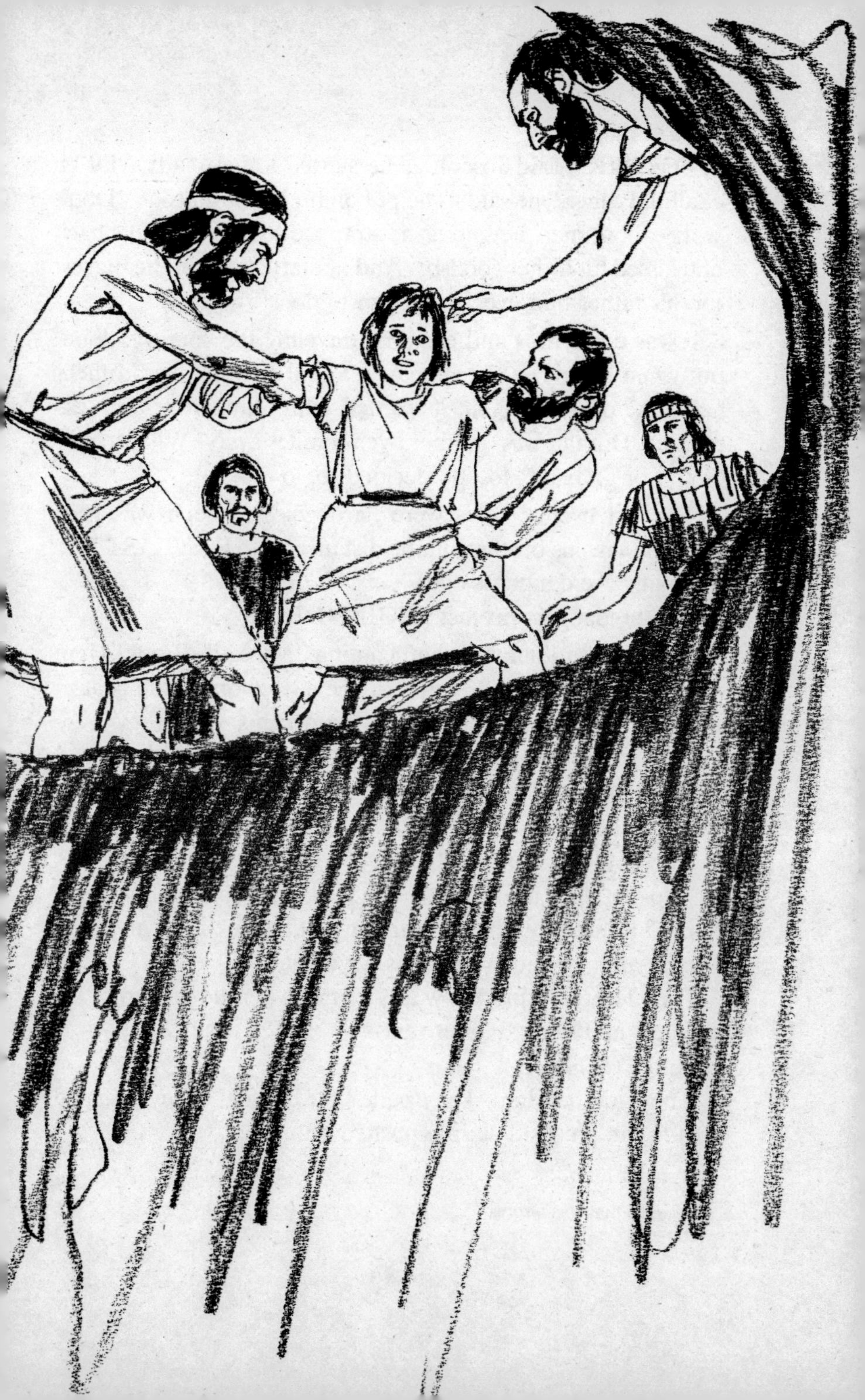

"Yes, SIR!" said Joseph as he started to get ready. "I'll be careful, Father," he said as he put on his beautiful coat. "Don't worry about me," he said as he strapped his lunch on his back and kissed his father good-by. And he started out on the biggest job his father had ever given him to do.

It was dangerous and exciting, traveling the country alone. But when he got to Shechem and found out that his brothers had gone on to Dothan, it seemed more dangerous and less exciting. Dothan was another twenty miles away! What to do? Go on or go back? Joseph decided to go on.

The last twenty miles were hard going. Joseph was glad when he saw his brothers in the distance. "Now—at LAST," he thought, "the danger is over."

But the danger was just BEGINNING.

When his brothers saw him coming, they said, "Look! Here comes the 'dreamer.'" They saw the gay colors of the coat in the distance. They remembered the dreams. And they were angry all over again.

"Let's kill him!" they said. "Let's throw him into a pit and say he was killed by a wild beast."

But the oldest brother, Reuben, had a twinge of conscience.*

"No—let's just throw him into a pit alive and leave him there to die," he said. But he was thinking, "I'll come back and save Joseph after my other brothers have gone."

Poor Joseph didn't know any of this when he ran up to his brothers and said, "Father sent—"

And THEN—

They grabbed him. They pulled off his coat. They dragged him to the pit. And—hup!—pushed him in!

---

* He knew that was wrong.

"Please—!" he called. But nobody answered. Had they gone off to leave him to die?

Joseph thought the end had come. And Reuben thought he would come back and save Joseph.

But they were BOTH wrong!

God had planned something ELSE—something neither of them had dreamed of!

LET'S TALK ABOUT THE BIBLE STORY

When Joseph got to Shechem he had a decision to make. What was it? How did he show that he was really obeying his father? Joseph obeyed his father and got into nothing but trouble. But there was a bright side; what was it?

A BIBLE VERSE TO LEARN

Children, obey your parents in all things. (Colossians 3:20, *KJV*)

LET'S TALK TO GOD

Dear God, help us to remember that you are taking care of us even when it doesn't LOOK that way. The important thing is for us to OBEY whether we get any thanks for it or not. Thank you for watching over our lives. In Jesus' name, Amen.

NOW FIND THIS STORY IN YOUR BIBLE

It's in Genesis 37:12–24.

STORY 18

THE JOURNEY THAT CHANGED A LIFE

Joseph was in the bottom of the pit where his brothers had thrown him. His brothers didn't answer when he shouted. His hands and feet slipped on the stones and sand as he tried to climb up. There was no way out. Joseph was in terrible trouble.

Now, if Joseph thought that things were pretty bad, he was mistaken. They weren't just bad. They were worse than that. They were TERRIBLE! Because Reuben was the only brother who wanted to save Joseph. And Reuben had gone away—perhaps to another meadow to watch some cattle. Joseph was alone in the pit. And the other brothers wanted to kill him.

ANYTHING could happen! And something did. Something that changed Joseph's whole life!

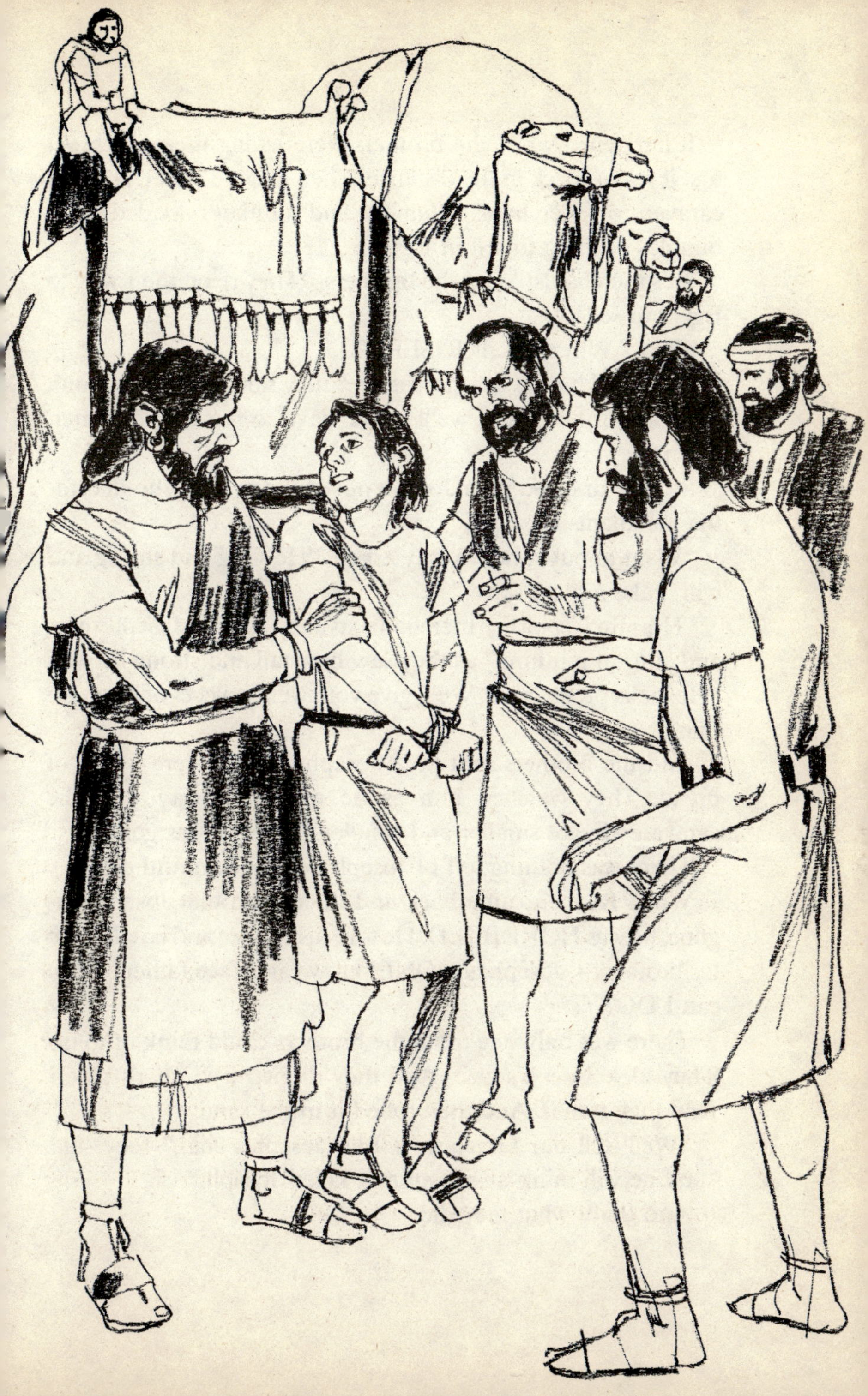

It happened while the brothers were eating their lunch. At first it was a speck in the distance. Then it came closer. It was a caravan of merchants. Camels and donkeys loaded with bundles of thing to sell in Egypt.

"It's merchants!" said the brothers. "They're on their way to Egypt to sell—"

SELL! Why not sell JOSEPH?

"Let's sell him to the merchants," they said. "Then we won't have to kill him. And we'll never have to see this 'dreamer' again."

So they dragged poor Joseph out of the pit and shouted for the merchants to stop.

"Want to buy a boy?" they asked. "He's big and strong and will make a good slave."

"Hmmm," said the merchants as they looked Joseph over, and "hummmmmm," as they saw how tall and strong he was. "He looks pretty good. We'll give you twenty pieces of silver for him."

And the brothers sold poor Joseph as if he were a loaf of bread. They watched him as he marched away with the caravan. He got smaller and smaller. Then he was gone.

There was nothing left of Joseph but his beautiful coat.

When Reuben came back and discovered that Joseph was gone, he was HORRIFIED. He tore his clothes and cried out to his brothers—"Joseph is GONE! How can I face father? What can I DO?"

There was only one thing the brothers could think of to do. They took Joseph's coat. And they dipped it in goat's blood. And they tore it. And they rolled it in the sand.

"We'll tell our father we found Joseph's coat," they said, "and he will think a wild animal killed Joseph."

And that's what they did.

"Well," they thought. "That's the end of Joseph!"

But it wasn't. They had forgotten one thing. They had forgotten God. God was still watching over Joseph. And there were some pretty exciting things ahead!

LET'S TALK ABOUT THE BIBLE STORY

There WAS something else the brothers could have done. What was it? When you've done something wrong, which is easier—to confess it or to try to "cover it up?" Which is right?

A BIBLE VERSE TO LEARN

Do not lie to one another. (Colossians 3:9, *NASB*)

LET'S TALK TO GOD

Dear God, help us to choose to do what's RIGHT when we are tempted to do wrong. But when we HAVE done something wrong, give us the courage to confess it and not go running around trying to cover it up. In Jesus' name, Amen.

NOW FIND THIS STORY IN YOUR BIBLE

It's in Genesis 37:25–31.

STORY 19

A TERRIBLE LIE

"Where's Joseph?"

Joseph's wicked brothers knew that would be the first thing their father Jacob would ask.

Where WAS Joseph?

Why, even his brothers didn't know for sure. They had sold him to a caravan of merchants, and he was gone off to Egypt—gone forever. There was nothing left of him but his beautiful coat. And that wasn't beautiful any more. The brothers had torn it and dipped it in blood.

A few days later the brothers started back home to their father Jacob. Where was Joseph? Well, it certainly looked like the end of him.

When the wicked brothers got home to their father, sure enough, the first thing he asked was, "Where's Joseph?"

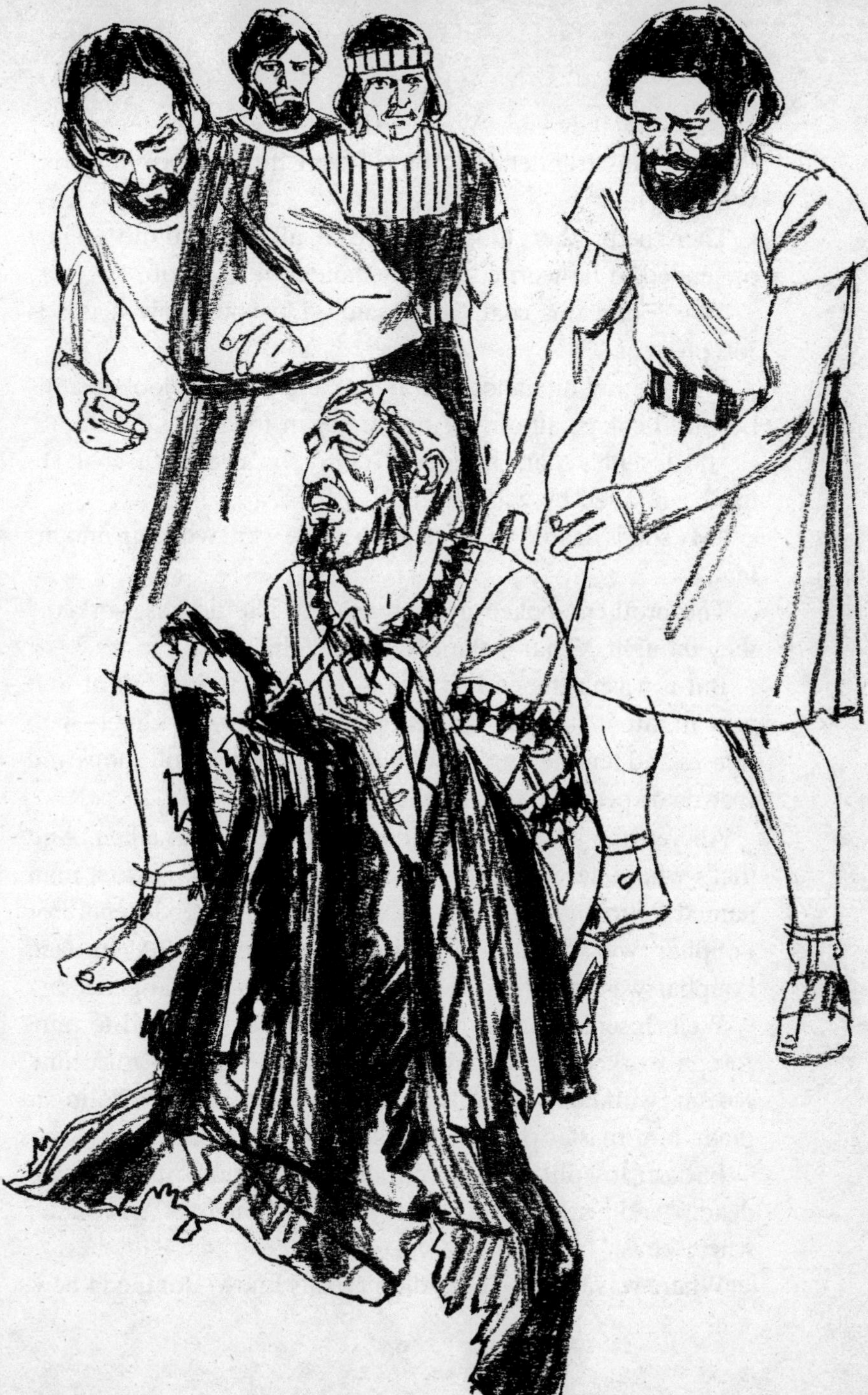

"Joseph?" they said. "We don't know. We haven't seen him."

Jacob was frightened. "Why, I sent him to look for you! Where is he?"

Then the brothers took out the coat, all torn and dirty. They pretended to be worried as they handed it to Jacob.

"We found this coat," they said. "Do you know if this is Joseph's coat?"

With trembling hands, Jacob took the coat. He looked at its beautiful colors, all dirty. And he began to cry.

"It's Joseph's coat," he cried. "It's my son's beautiful coat. He has been killed by wild animals!"

"My son is dead!" he moaned. And he went weeping into his tent.

The brothers looked at each other. "The lie has worked," they thought. "That is the end of Joseph."

But it wasn't the end—it was a new beginning! For at that very moment Joseph was being taken to Egypt. Egypt—with houses and temples instead of tents! And streets and shops and crowds of people! And a slave market!

Ah yes, the slave market. That's where he was taken. And that's where he was SOLD. He was sold as a slave, to a man named Potiphar. But God was still watching over Joseph. For Potiphar was rich. And Potiphar was important. In fact, Potiphar was an officer of the King! And what happened?

Well, Joseph worked hard, and Potiphar was kind to him. Joseph worked harder still, and Potiphar began to trust him. Joseph worked harder than EVER—and finally—Potiphar made him master over all the other slaves in his house!

Back in Joseph's own country, his father thought, "Joseph is dead." And his wicked brothers secretly thought, "We wonder where he is."

Where was Joseph? They didn't really know. But God knew.

And God knew, too, that He was going to be with Joseph every minute!

LET'S TALK ABOUT THE BIBLE STORY

How is God showing that he is still watching over Joseph? Do you suppose Joseph believes that he is? How is Joseph showing it?

A BIBLE VERSE TO LEARN

Do not fear, for I am with you;. . . I will help you. (Isaiah 41:10, *NASB*)

LET'S TALK TO GOD

Dear God, even when everything is going WRONG, help us to show that we still believe you, by OBEYING cheerfully instead of going off in a corner and SULKING. And help us to always remember that you are with us. In Jesus' name, Amen.

NOW FIND THIS STORY IN YOUR BIBLE

It's in Genesis 37:31-36.

STORY 20

THE DREAM THAT WAS ALMOST FORGOTTEN

The Lord was with Joseph in Potiphar's house. Potiphar was kind to Joseph and made him captain over all his slaves. And then something happened to spoil it all!

It was another lie. This time it was Potiphar's wife who told the lie. She told Potiphar that Joseph had done something very wicked. And Potiphar believed her and put Joseph in—of all places—PRISON!

This was REAL trouble. But Joseph had been in trouble before, and by this time he knew that the best thing to do in trouble was to behave himself. He worked hard, and the jailer was kind to him. He worked harder still, and the jailer began to trust him. He worked harder than EVER—and the jailer made him captain over all the other prisoners!

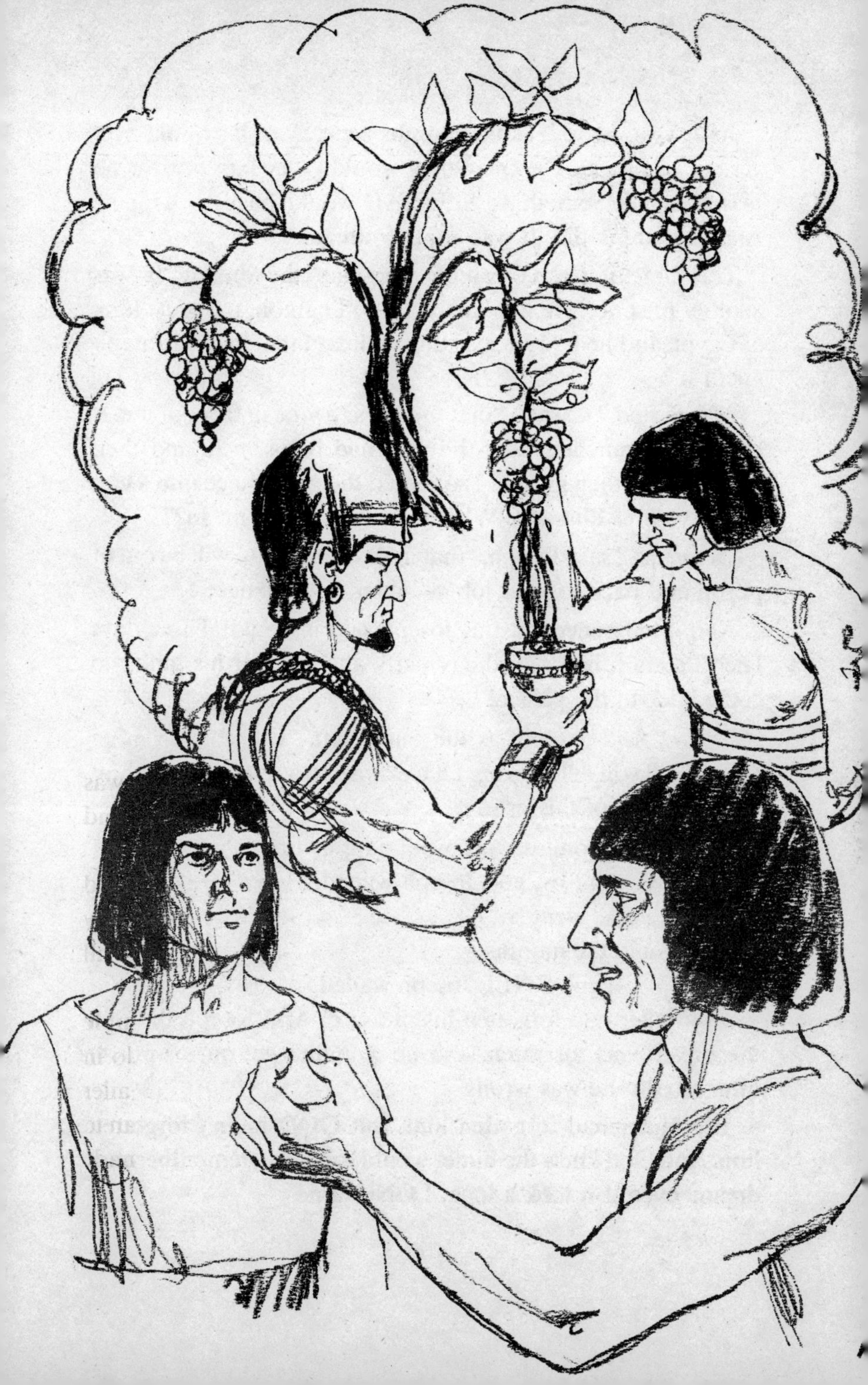

Joseph wondered, as the months went by, if he would ever get out of prison. He knew they wouldn't let him out for no reason at all. Something SPECIAL would have to happen. And something did. It was another dream.

This time it wasn't Joseph who had the dream. It was another prisoner. He was the butler to Pharaoh, the great king of Egypt, and he had such a strange dream that he told Joseph about it.

"I dreamed," he said, "that there was a vine in front of me. It had three branches. First the vine had buds on it, and then flowers—and then grapes! I squeezed the grape juice into a cup and gave it to Pharaoh. What does this dream mean?"

"It means," said Joseph, "that in three days you will be out of prison and back to your job as butler in the palace."

And it happened—just as Joseph said it would! Three days later, Pharaoh had a birthday party and sent for his butler to come back to the palace!

"Now," said Joseph, as the butler left, "will you do me a favor? Will you tell the king I have done no wrong, and ask him to get me out of this prison?"

The butler promised and went happily on his way.

The days went by, and Joseph waited.

    The weeks went by,

        and the months—

            and STILL Joseph waited.

The butler had forgotten his promise! And Joseph thought the dream was forgotten, and he wouldn't get out of prison after all. But he was wrong.

The butler had forgotten him. But GOD hadn't forgotten him. And God knew the butler would some day remember that dream, even if it took a long, LONG time.

LET'S TALK ABOUT THE BIBLE STORY
Things look pretty grim for Joseph, don't they? He's depending on somebody's promise, to get out of prison. Whose? Do you think that might be a mistake? Why? Can people always keep their promises? Does God? Who is really watching over Joseph—God or the butler?

A BIBLE VERSE TO LEARN
God is with you. He will not fail you nor forsake you. (1 Chronicles 28:20, *NASB*)

LET'S TALK TO GOD
Dear God, we know that some people don't keep their promises because they WON'T and some people don't keep their promises because they CAN'T. But you always keep your promises no matter what. Thank you for watching over Joseph. And thank you for watching over us. In Jesus' name, Amen.

NOW FIND THIS STORY IN YOUR BIBLE
It's in Genesis 39:1–23 and 40:1–23.

STORY 21

THE DREAM THAT SET A PRISONER FREE

God had not forgotten Joseph. God knew that the butler would remember the dream, even if it took a long time.

Joseph waited for weeks. He waited for months. He waited and waited—until TWO WHOLE YEARS went by!

And then a strange thing happened. It was another dream.

This time it was Pharaoh, the king of Egypt, who had the dream. It was a strange dream, and none of Pharaoh's wise men could tell what it meant. Then—at last—the butler remembered Joseph. And the dream. And his promise! Right then and there he told the Pharaoh that Joseph could tell him what his dream meant. "Send for him," cried the Pharaoh, "at once!"

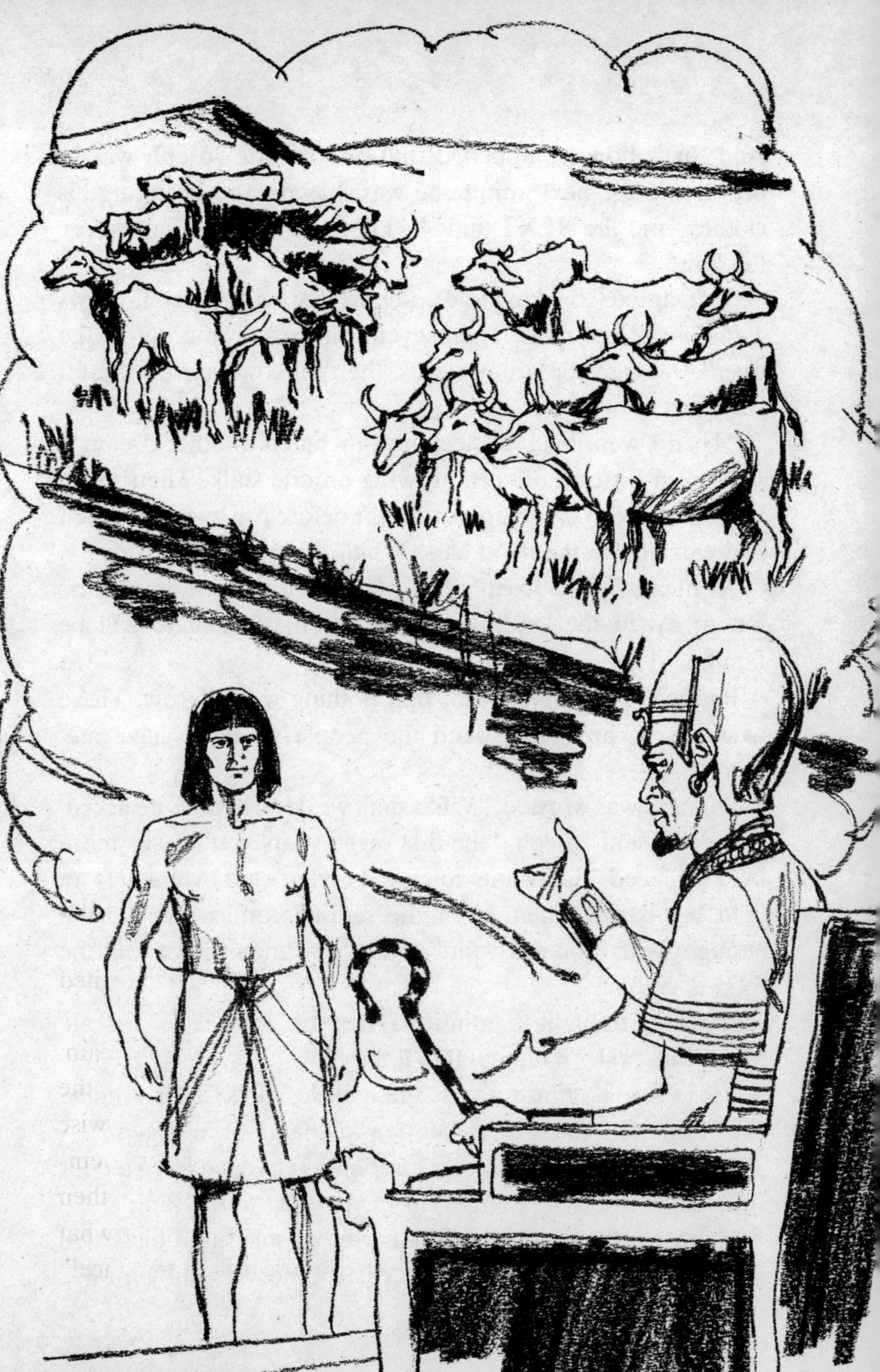

And that's how it happened that one minute Joseph was in prison and the next minute he was shaving and changing his clothes—and the NEXT thing he knew, he was standing before the king!

"I dreamed," the king told Joseph, "that I saw seven fat cows come out of the river. Then seven thin cows came out of the river. And right before my eyes, the thin cows ate up the fat cows.

"Then I went back to sleep and dreamed another dream. I saw seven fat ears of corn growing on one stalk. Then seven bad ears of corn came up. And right before my eyes, the seven bad ears ate up the good ears. What does it mean?"

"It means," said Joseph, "that for seven years there will be lots to eat in the land. Then—for seven years there will be famine."

Famine! Why that meant that nothing would grow. There wouldn't be any grain. And the people wouldn't have any food!

Pharaoh was worried. "What shall we do, Joseph?" he asked.

"Well," said Joseph, "the first seven years you'll have more than you need. God wants you to save what's left over and store it in big barns. Then when the famine comes, you'll have enough food. You must find a very wise man to see that the food is saved."

Pharaoh thought a minute. Then he looked at Joseph. "You," he said. "You are JUST the man."

Paraoh took off his ring. He put it on Joseph's finger. And he said, "I hereby make you the man in charge of all Egypt."

Just like that. In a moment, Joseph was changed from a poor prisoner to the head man in all Egypt, next to the king!

He traveled over Egypt, making the people build big barns and store food. He lived in a palace. And nobody in Egypt was more powerful than Joseph, except the king. At last things were going well with Joseph!

Yes, it took a long time. But God was certainly watching over Joseph, every step of the way.

LET'S TALK ABOUT THE BIBLE STORY

Well, Joseph waited a long time before he found out what God was up to, didn't he? Can you remember some of the things that happened to get Joseph to Egypt? Why do you suppose God did it in such a roundabout way? Why didn't he just let Joseph get on a camel and go be the head man in Egypt without going to all that trouble?

A BIBLE VERSE TO LEARN

Have faith in God. (Mark 11:22, *KJV*)

LET'S TALK TO GOD

Dear God, it takes such a long time to grow up and be wise and strong. Help us to be willing to learn every little lesson along the way. Help us not to be in too much of a hurry. In Jesus' name, Amen.

NOW FIND THIS STORY IN YOUR BIBLE

It's in Genesis 41:1-49.

STORY 22

AN OLD DREAM THAT CAME TRUE

God had thought of everything. Joseph was ruler over all Egypt, next to the king. For seven years, he made the people store food in big barns. And then the Pharaoh's dream began to come true.

Famine!

Just as Joseph had said, the grain didn't grow—and there wasn't any food anywhere—except in the big barns. People came from all over the country to buy food. They came from other countries too, for the famine was all over the land.

And then, one day—another dream began to come true. It was Joseph's own dream—the one he'd had so many years before! And this is how it happened.

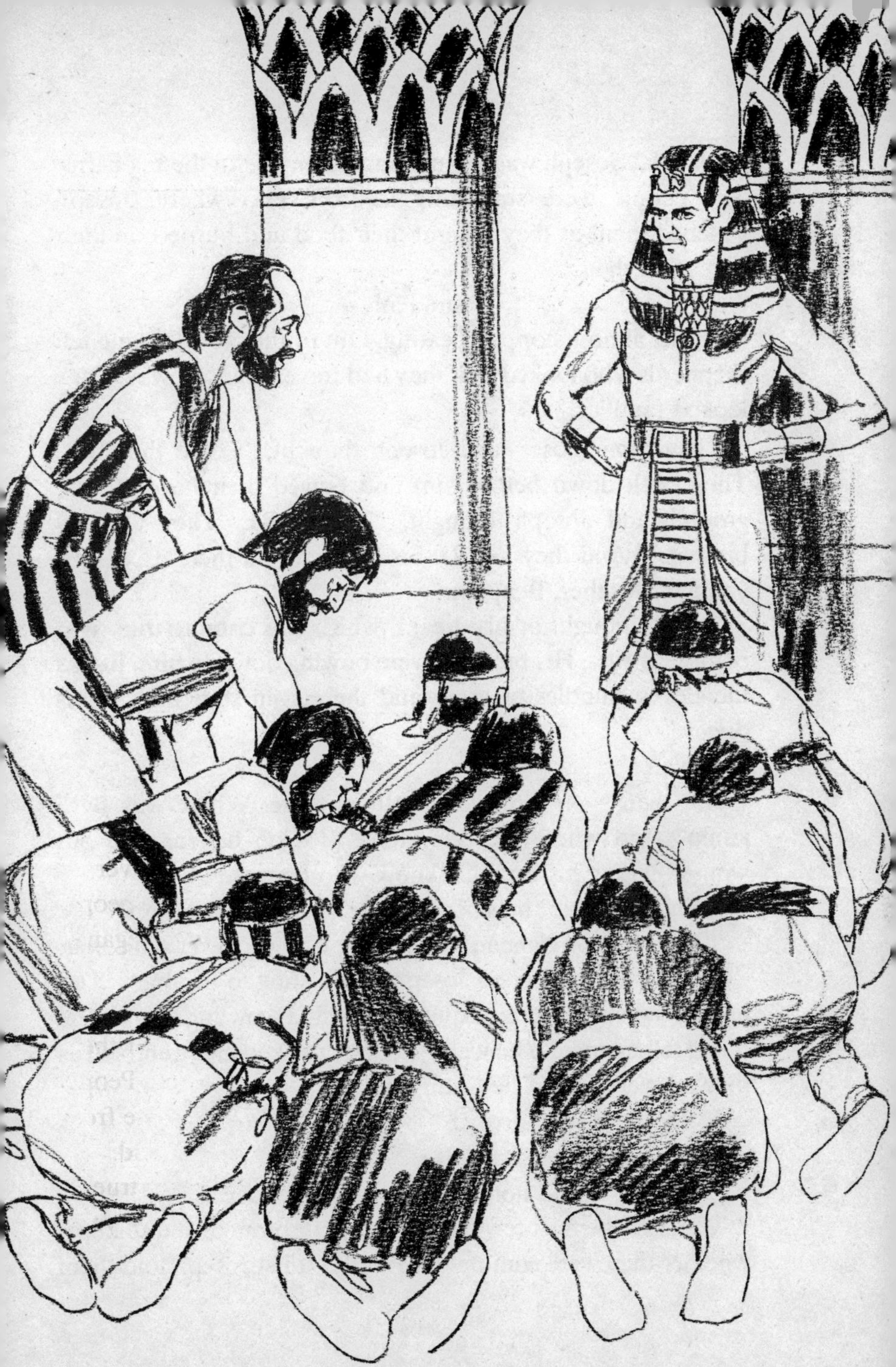

One day Joseph was selling grain from one of the big barns. The people were streaming in from everywhere. Joseph watched them as they bought their food and hurried on their way. And then—

suddenly—

his heart almost stopped beating. Out of the crowds came ten shepherds who looked as if they had traveled a long way. They looked familiar.

They came closer—and Joseph thought, "Could they be?" They knelt down before him and bowed their heads to the ground—and Joseph thought, "They ARE. They are my brothers!" And they WERE his brothers—all there except his youngest brother, Benjamin.

Joseph thought of his dream, which was coming true right before his eyes. His brothers were bowing down to him, just as the eleven bundles of grain and the eleven stars had, in his dream!

Eleven.

But there were only ten brothers there. Where was Benjamin? And where was his father? Joseph had to find out without letting his brothers know who he was.

"Who are you?" he said. "Where do you come from?"

"We are from Canaan," they said, bowing lower than ever.

"You are spies!" cried Joseph, pretending to be angry. And he asked them all sorts of questions with a scowling face but he didn't tell them who he was. And they quaked and trembled as they answered. And he found out—

Benjamin was alive.

His father was alive.

And none of them had any food.

Well, for the next few days, those poor brothers didn't know whether they were coming or GOING. First Joseph told them

108

he would send one of them home to get their brother Benjamin while the rest of them waited in Egypt. Then he put them all in prison! THEN—at the end of three days, he told them they could ALL go home but Simeon. By this time they were thoroughly confused and very frightened.

"Leave Simeon here," he said. "The rest of you go home and take some food, but bring your youngest brother back. Then I'll know if you're telling the truth."

"This is what we deserve," said the brothers, "for selling poor Joseph to be a slave and for telling our father a lie." They spoke in their own language. They didn't think the great Egyptian ruler could understand them.

But the great Egyptian ruler DID understand them. For he was their own brother Joseph.

God had provided food, even for the wicked brothers. But before they got home, they were in for a surprise. And God was going to make the REST of Joseph's dream come true, too!

LET'S TALK ABOUT THE BIBLE STORY

Joseph was certainly hard on his brothers. He put them through three or four very bad days. Why do you suppose he did this? How do you suppose the brothers felt when they had to leave Simeon behind in prison? Underneath all this trouble, was God's kindness. What had God really done for the wicked brothers? Whom did He use to do this?

A BIBLE VERSE TO LEARN

Give thanks to the Lord, for He is good. (Psalm 136:1, *NASB*)

LET'S TALK TO GOD

Dear God, you went to a great deal of trouble to take care of Joseph, and then used Joseph to take care of his father and brothers. We thank you that you watch over us, even though we can't always understand what you are doing or why. In Jesus' name, Amen.

NOW FIND THIS STORY IN YOUR BIBLE
It's in Genesis 41:53–57 and 42:1–24.

STORY 23

THE JOURNEY WITH NINE SURPRISES

When Joseph's brothers started back home, they didn't know they had nine surprises. Their donkeys were loaded up to their long ears with sacks of grain. As the brothers traveled along, they were half-happy and half-frightened. They were happy because they had food. And frightened because they'd had to leave Simeon behind in prison. They wondered how they were going to tell their father Jacob.

When night came and the desert pulled long shadows up over its toes to get ready for bed, the brothers stopped to rest. And that's when they found the first surprise. One of them opened a sack of grain to feed the donkeys—and stopped and stared. "My moneybag," he said. "It's full of money." He dumped it out and counted it. "I used all my money to pay for the food," he said. "But it's all here. Every bit."

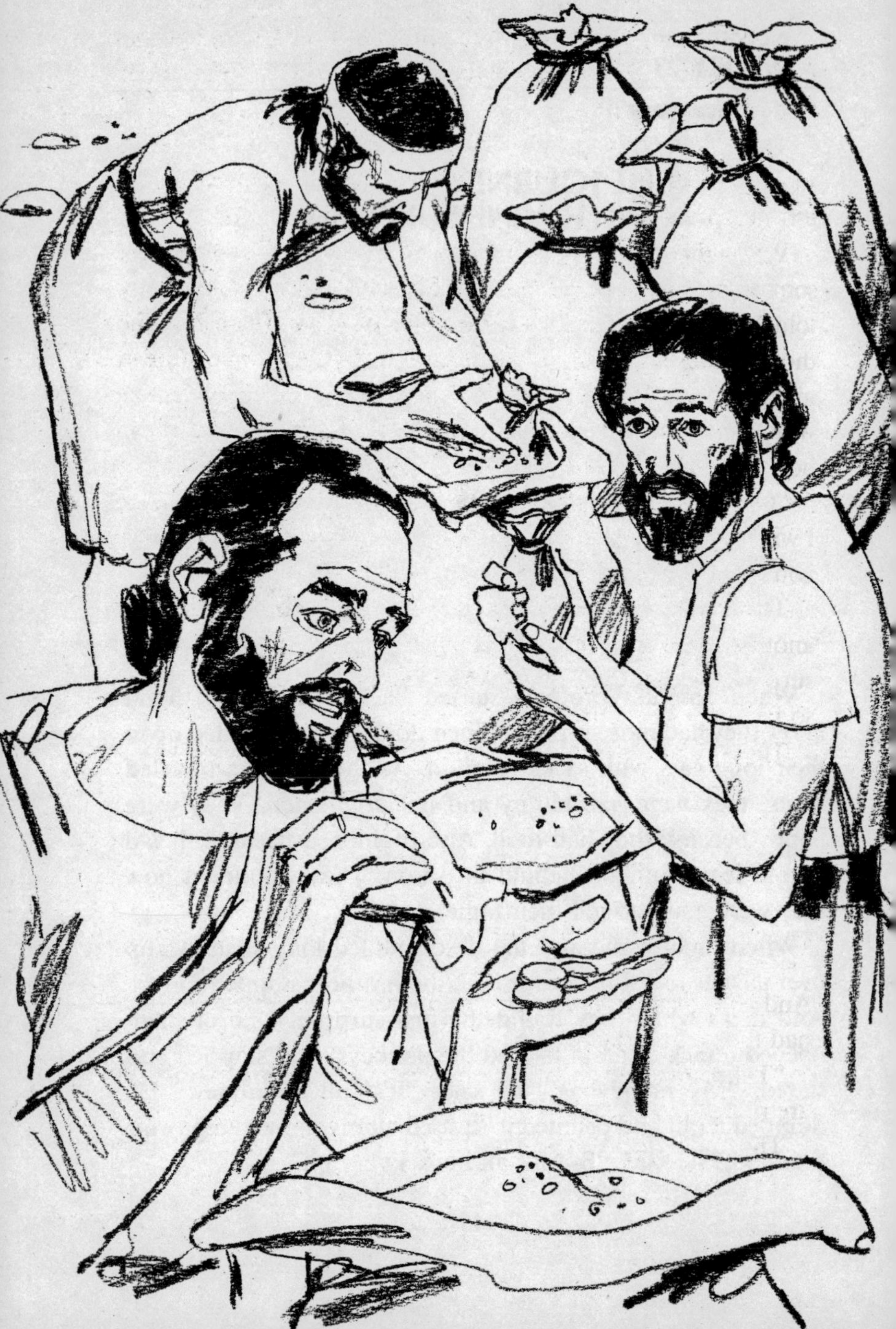

Nobody knew what to say for a minute. Then they all began to talk at once. "The ruler will think you STOLE it," they cried. "What shall we do?"

There was nothing they COULD do. They went to sleep, more frightened than they'd ever been in their lives. And in the morning they went on with their journey.

When they got home, their father Jacob knew at once that something was wrong. "Where's Simeon?" he said. And they told him everything. About the ruler of Egypt. And how he thought they were wicked men. And made them leave Simeon in prison. And asked them to bring Benjamin back, so he would know they were telling the truth. And they told Jacob how they had found the money.

"Oh, Simeon!" wailed Jacob. And, "Oh, my poor Benjamin! I will not send him to Egypt. He may be killed. See the trouble you have got us in!"

The brothers didn't know what to say. They began to unpack another donkey. And that's when they found the second surprise. Another bag of money! Then they unpacked donkeys so fast their heads were spinning.

Three donkeys—
  four—
    five—
      six—
        seven—
          eight—
           NINE!

And nine bags of money! Every bit of the money the brothers had taken with them!

"The ruler of Egypt will think we are thieves," they said. "We are really in trouble."

The nine surprises made them very frightened. But they

didn't know the ruler of Egypt was Joseph. They didn't know he returned good for evil and gave them surprises as gifts. And they didn't know that—the biggest surprise was yet to come!

LET'S TALK ABOUT THE BIBLE STORY

What did Joseph do to return good for evil? How did the brothers feel when they found the nine surprises? What are some ways in our own lives that we can return good for evil? It isn't easy to do by ourselves; who can help us?

A BIBLE VERSE TO LEARN

Love your enemies, do good to those who hate you. (Luke 6:27, *NASB*)

LET'S TALK TO GOD

Dear God, it isn't always easy to be nice to people after they've been mean to us. We need your help. We know it is one way of showing you that we love you. Please help us to remember this. In Jesus' name, Amen.

NOW FIND THIS STORY IN YOUR BIBLE

It's in Genesis 42:25-38.

STORY 24

THE BIGGEST SURPRISE OF ALL

Joseph's brothers and their father Jacob had food. But they were sad. Because Simeon was in prison in Egypt. And the ruler thought they were thieves.

When it was time to go back for more food, they were sadder still. Because poor Benjamin had to go with them. "You MUST let us take Benjamin," the brothers told Jacob, "or the ruler won't even see us." And poor Jacob had to let Benjamin go.

But when they got back to Egypt, they had MORE surprises waiting for them.

They took Benjamin up to the great ruler, and stood there trembling. And then they had the first surprise. Instead of putting them in prison, the ruler told his servant to take them to his palace for dinner! "Now we ARE in trouble," they thought. "He's going to make us all his slaves."

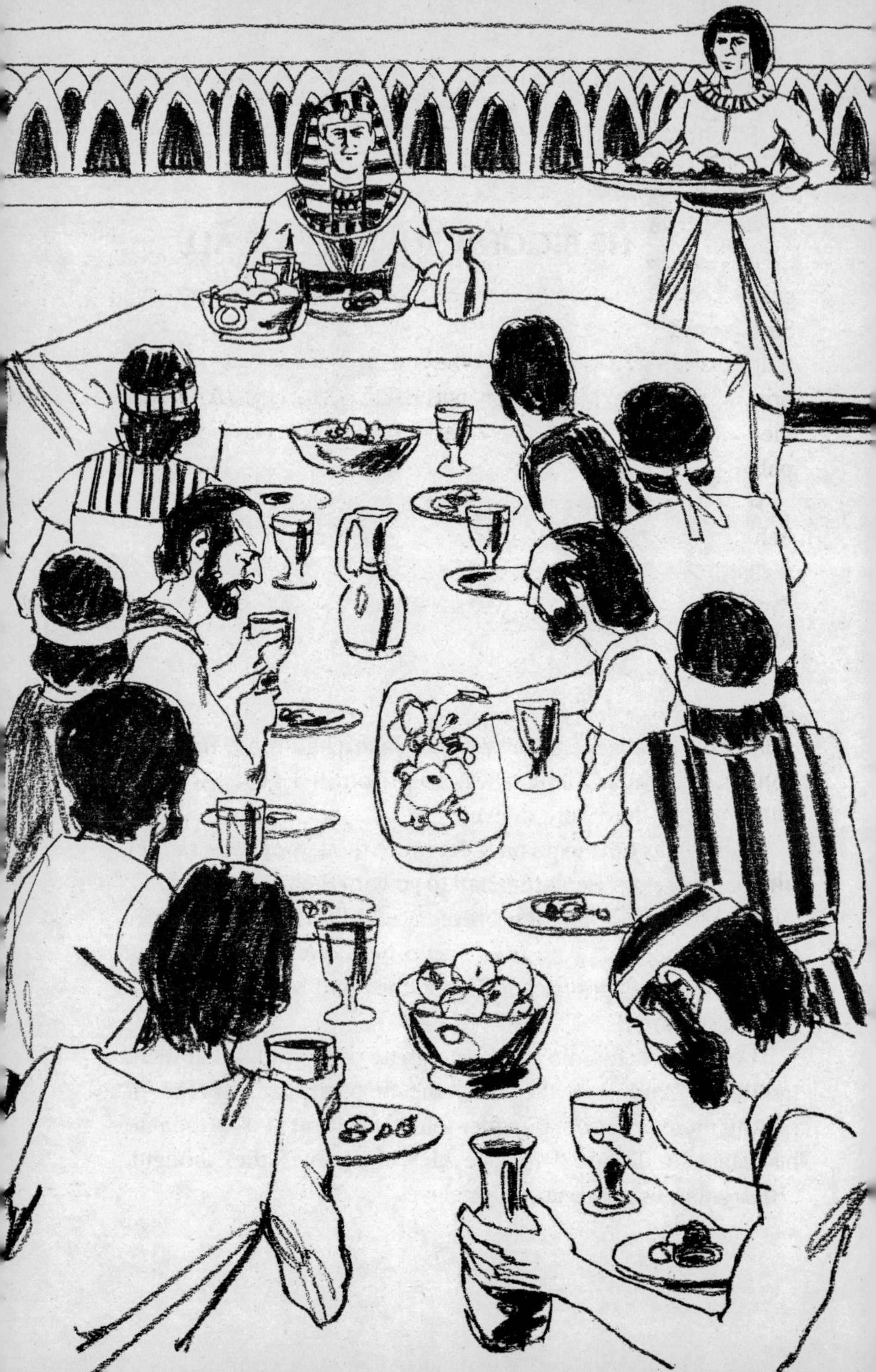

When they got to the palace, the brothers tried to explain to the ruler's head servant. "We found the money in our sacks," they said. "We didn't steal it."

The servant smiled. "It must have been God who put the money in your sacks," he said. "I received the money for your grain." And before they could get over that surprise, he brought Simeon out to them.

It was all so topsy-turvy! They all expected to be put IN prison—and instead, Simeon was OUT of prison. And here they all were, safe and sound, and about to have dinner in a palace!

When the great ruler came in, the brothers all bowed down before him.

"Is this your young brother?" the ruler asked. They told him "yes"—and they were too frightened to notice that the ruler had tears in his eyes.

The brothers were frightened all through dinner, and frightened right up until the next surprise. The ruler ordered their donkeys packed with grain and said that the brothers could go home! The poor brothers were quite dizzy with surprises by this time.

Early the next morning they started for home, feeling that they'd had the strangest adventure of their lives. But the surprises weren't over yet.

The brothers hadn't gone very far, when the ruler's chief servant hurried after them. "The ruler's silver cup is missing," he cried. "Why have you stolen it?"

The poor brothers said they hadn't stolen anything, but they were frightened. They unloaded their donkeys—and there was the silver cup—in Benjamin's sack! With heavy hearts,* they

---

*This means they were afraid.

went back to Egypt and bowed again before the great ruler.

"Please don't punish Benjamin," they begged. "Our poor father will die. Keep one of us as your slave, but let Benjamin go!" Imagine! The same men who sold their brother Joseph, were willing to do anything to save their brother Benjamin now! And Joseph knew they had learned their lesson. They weren't wicked any more. He was ready to give them the biggest surprise of all!

"Look at me," he said, "I am your brother Joseph."

Well, THAT surprise was almost too great to believe. They just stared.

"I AM," said Joseph. "Don't be afraid of me. And don't be sorry you sold me as a slave. God has made me ruler of Egypt, so that I could provide you with food. And then he hugged Benjamin, right before their eyes, and they knew he was telling the truth.

Oh, joy! It was almost too much to believe. Joseph forgave them for the wrong they had done! They all laughed and talked and cried together and thanked God for the biggest surprise of all! They were all together again!

LET'S TALK ABOUT THE BIBLE STORY

Joseph's brothers were actually being watched and tested, weren't they? Who was testing them? In what way did they show that they had learned their lesson? Can you think of some people who watch your life to see if you are the Christian you SAY you are?

A BIBLE VERSE TO LEARN

Even a child is known by his doings, whether his work be pure, and whether it be right. (Proverbs 20:11, *KJV*)

LET'S TALK TO GOD

Dear God, we thank you for giving us another chance to learn our lesson when we've made a mistake. Help us to remember that other people watch our lives. Help us to give them something GOOD to watch. In Jesus' name, Amen.

NOW FIND THIS STORY IN YOUR BIBLE

It's in Genesis 43:1–34 and 44:1–34 and 45:1–15.

STORY 25

THE BEST NEWS OF ALL

Joseph was together with his brothers at last. Oh, joy! That was the best surprise of all. There was only one thing missing. Joseph wanted to see his father Jacob and tell him the good news.

Joseph and his brothers shared their surprise with everybody. And the news traveled fast. When it reached Pharaoh, the king of Egypt, he sent for Joseph. "Tell your brothers to go home and get all their families. And your father. And come back here to LIVE. Give them extra donkeys and food and wagons—everything they need."

Oh, joy! Now the surprise was almost complete!

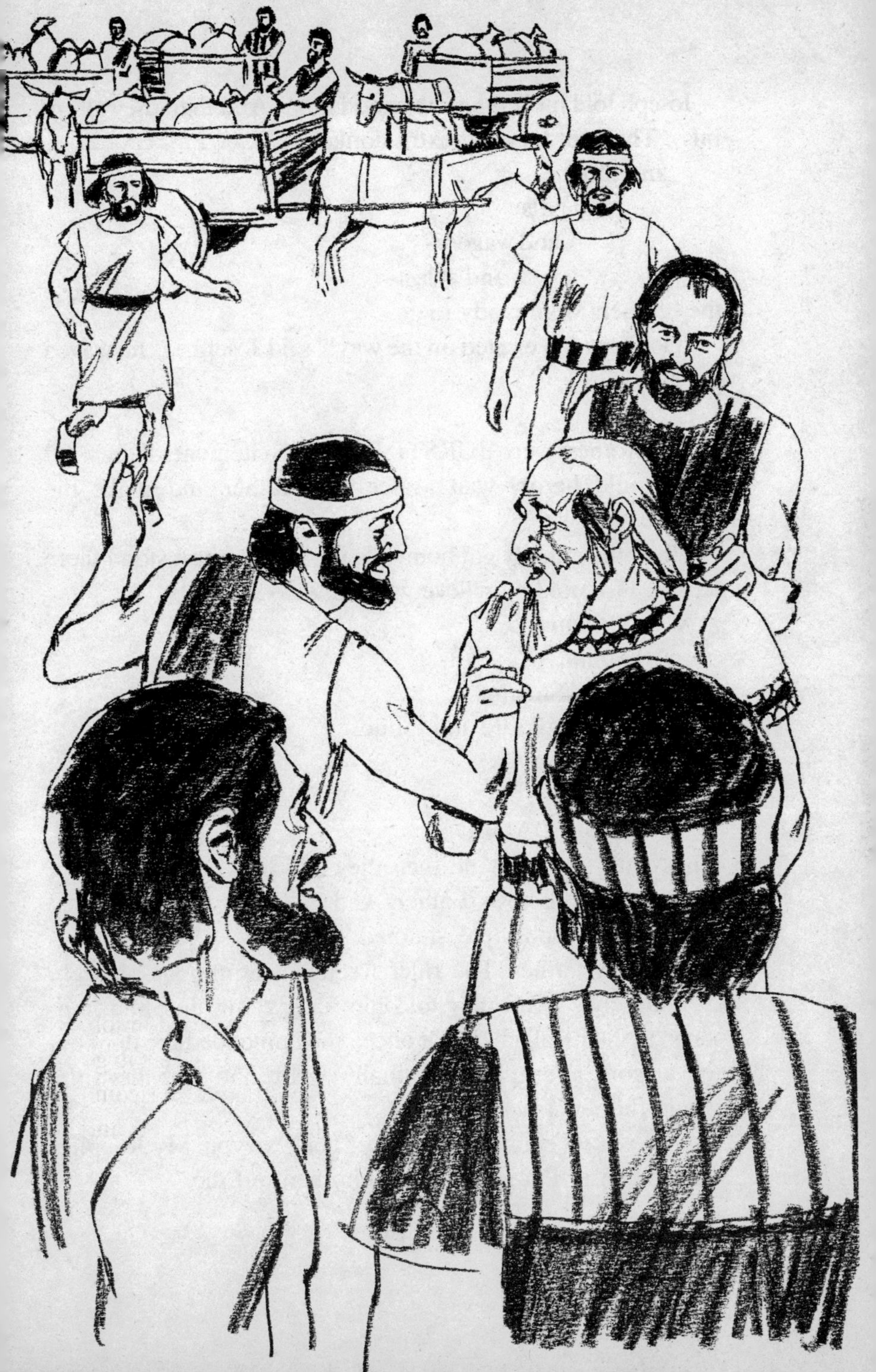

Joseph told his brothers the good news. And then they all got busy. They got together extra donkeys
    and food
        and gifts
            and wagons—
                and at last—
the brothers were ready to go.

"Don't get too excited on the way!" said Joseph, as he waved good-by.

Excited!

The brothers were BURSTING with excitement all the way! They could hardly wait to see their father and make the surprise complete.

When they finally got home, dear old Jacob just stood there staring. He couldn't believe what he saw—his sons.

ALL of them.
    Benjamin.
        And Simeon.
            All safe and sound.
With extra donkeys.
    And wagons.
        Just LOADED.
What could this be? And then they told him.

"Joseph is still alive, Father. And he's ruler of all Egypt!"

Jacob just stood there, stunned.

"It's true, Father. The ruler we told you about is Joseph. OUR Joseph." And they told him everything that had happened to them—all talking at once. They unloaded the donkeys and wagons and gifts. And finally Jacob had to believe the wonderful news.

"You've said enough," he cried. "I believe you. My Joseph is still alive. And I'm going to see him before I die."

And then they all began to talk about it. They talked about it while the hillside covered itself up with shadows for the night. They talked about it while the donkeys got sleepy. They talked about it far into the night. And then they dreamed about it, while God watched over them.

For they were all going back to Egypt to make the surprise complete. And Joseph was going to see the one he loved best of all—his dear old father Jacob!

LET'S TALK ABOUT THE BIBLE STORY

Joseph was rich and popular and famous now, but he did not forget one important thing. What was it? What did he do to honor his father? How did that make Jacob feel?

A BIBLE VERSE TO LEARN

Honor your father and your mother. (Exodus 20:12, *NASB*)

LET'S TALK TO GOD

Dear God, help us to remember what you say in the Bible—"Honor your father and your mother." Help us to honor them not just when we NEED them—but when we're popular and busy, too. In Jesus' name, Amen.

NOW FIND THIS STORY IN YOUR BIBLE

It's in Genesis 45:9–28.

STORY 26

A WISH THAT CAME TRUE

Jacob could hardly wait to see his son Joseph. "Joseph, Joseph," he thought, as the families took down the tents and rolled up the rugs and loaded the donkeys and camels for the journey. "My Joseph," he thought, as they gathered the cattle and got ready to leave. "Joseph," his heart sang as he climbed into a wagon and they finally started. "Joseph—Jo-o-o-seph," the wagon wheels seemed to say as they creaked along.

Jacob counted the days. It was so hard to wait! He thought about how OLD he was, and wondered if he'd live to get there safely. He wondered—right up until he had the dream. One night when they stopped to rest, Jacob thanked God for taking care of them and went to sleep.

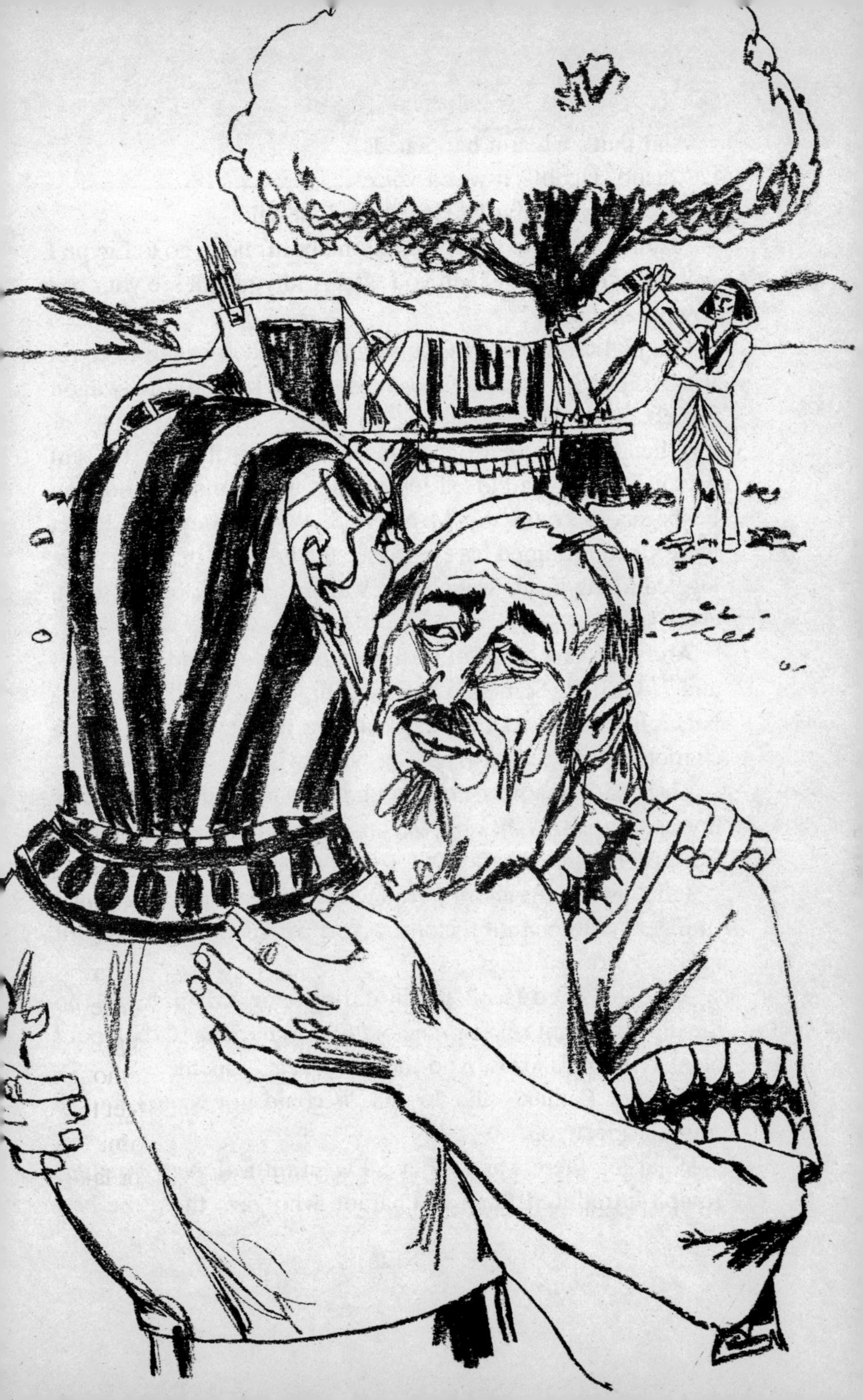

And that's when it happened.

"Jacob, Jacob!" It was a voice!

Jacob listened hard. "Here I am," he said.

"I am God," said the voice. "Don't be afraid to go to Egypt. I will be with you and keep you safe. And you will see your son Joseph again."

Oh, joy! Oh wonder! God was good! Jacob began to count the HOURS. "Joseph, J-o-o-o-seph," creaked the wagon wheels.

When they got near Egypt, Jacob could hardly wait. He sent his son Judah ahead to tell Joseph they were coming. And then he began to count the MINUTES. Would they EVER get there? Jacob strained his eyes to see the first sign of Egypt as he joggled along in his wagon. He watched every cloud of dust, every speck.

And then one cloud of dust became a speck and got bigger and BIGGER. Someone was coming. Was it Judah coming back? Jacob looked HARD. Was it a donkey? No—it was a chariot. A big, beautiful chariot with swift horses and—who?

The chariot came nearer, and Jacob held his breath. The horses stopped by Jacob's wagon, their coats wet and shining from running hard, and sent a swirl of dust up around them.

Judah was in the chariot. And with him was a tall, handsome stranger. With beautiful clothes. And a gold chain around his neck. The ruler of Egypt.

"Joseph!" cried Jacob, hardly daring to believe his eyes. And the big important ruler sprang out of the chariot and took poor old Jacob in his arms. And they both cried together.

"Father, Father," said Joseph, "I could not wait. I had to come to meet you."

What joy there was as they all went on to Egypt together! Joseph introduced them to Pharaoh who gave them the best part of the land to live in. All the surprises were complete at last.

And God had been watching over them all—every minute!

LET'S TALK ABOUT THE BIBLE STORY

How did God let poor old Jacob know that He was with him? Do you remember another dream Jacob had when he was a young man?* What was the very last surprise? Do you think God is with you when you go on trips? How do you know? Where in the Bible does it say so?

A BIBLE VERSE TO LEARN

The LORD has done great things for us; we are glad. (Psalm 126:3, *NASB*)

LET'S TALK TO GOD

Dear God, we know you are always watching over us. Even though we don't have dreams or hear voices or see angels or things like that. You have told us so in the Bible. Help us to remember this. And thank you. In Jesus' name, Amen.

NOW FIND THIS STORY IN YOUR BIBLE

It's in Genesis 46:1-34 and 47:1-12.

---

* It's in story 13.

God's Word

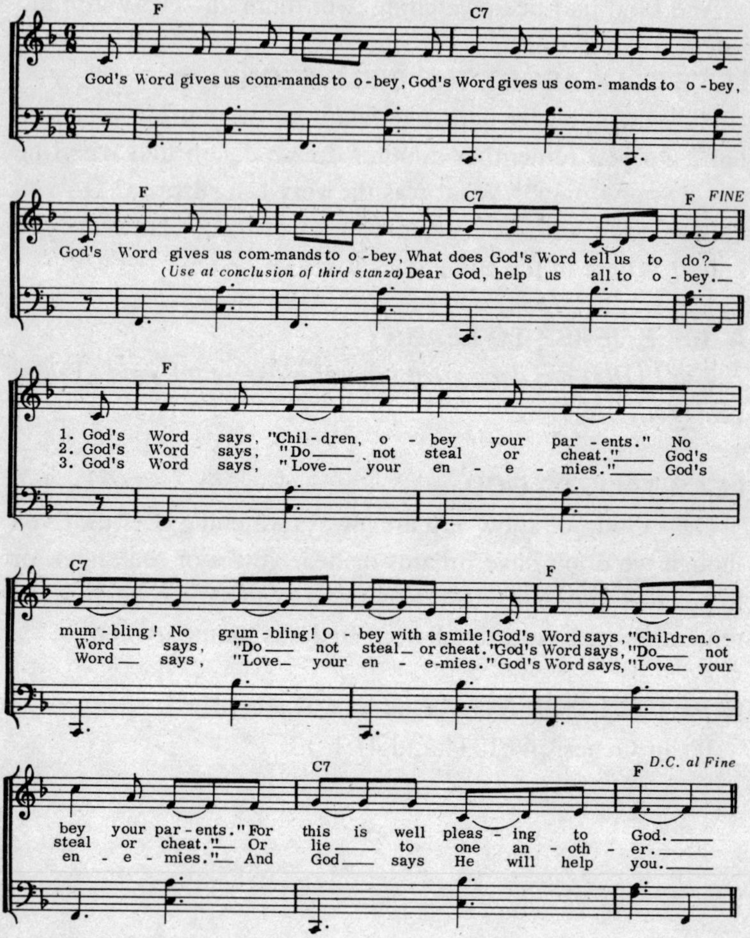

Words: Margaret M. Self. Music: Traditional.